"You can downloa
monkeywithapin.com. And
explains to you exactly w
managers you hire to run yo
make the kind of returns studies show the equity market is
supposed to offer."
Merryn Somerset Webb, Editor-in-Chief, MoneyWeek

"The universal reaction after reading this book is going to be,
I wish I had read it years ago, and mine was no exception.
Being completely detached from the finance industry, and a
seasoned researcher trained to sift fact from mantra, gives
Pete Comley a unique vantage point of the industry -
everything in the book is based on solid evidence, and will
save you from being ripped off by the "professionals" every
step of the way.
There is no agenda, theme or conjecture; just plain facts that
most of us simply don't know and are blissfully kept in the
dark about. This is certainly the best book I have ever read on
the subject, and no one even remotely connected with money
matters can afford to ignore it."
Amazon reader review from a private investor
(Noor Ahmed)

"It's a marvellous book, and will be right up there near the
top of my UK recommended books for investing. Comley's
book is so thorough, it's something all financial advisors
should read."

George Kinder, The Kinder Institute of Life Planning

About the author:
Pete Comley

Pete is a private investor who has been trading shares for over a decade. He has a degree in psychology and he has worked for most of his career in market research. He's well known within that industry as a conference speaker and also an innovator.

He was the first person to run commercial online surveys in the UK in the mid-1990s. Pete founded his own market research company in 1998 and now works part time for them.

Apart from investing, Pete's other interests include gardening, and he recently created allotments in his local village for 150 people. He also runs fungi identification courses and is in the process of walking the entire coast of England and Wales with his wife.

Pete can be contacted on twitter: @petecomley or by email: pete.comley@monkeywithapin.com.

Monkey with a Pin

Why you may be missing 6% a year from your investment returns

Pete Comley

.

Disclaimers:

- This document is meant for personal use only.
- All content in this book is meant for informational and educational purposes only and does not constitute professional advice.
- All information is to be accepted on an "as is" basis with no warranty expressed or implied as to its accuracy or reliability.
- In no event will the author or publisher be liable for any loss or damage resulting from the use of the material.
- The information within the book is not intended as a substitute for any legal, financial or other professional advice. In the event that such services are required, you should seek the guidance of a qualified and competent professional.

By reading past this point, you shall accept these terms.

Contents

Preface

The initial idea for this book came to me one day in early May 2011 while I was on my new allotment. I was digging away and listening to a podcast by the eminent David Kuo of The Motley Fool UK,[1] who was talking to one of the contestants in The Share Centre's Shares4Schools competition.

David:

OK. Now here is something that I found quite interesting, because I went on the website just to have a look to see how your school has done compared to the other 72 schools in the competition. Eleven of the 72 schools have beaten the market. Over the seven-month period, the market has gone up 5%, so approximately 15% of the schools have beaten the market. The other 85%, which includes your school, have not beaten the market. So what does that, first of all, tell you about stock picking?

Grant:

Well, in the short term, it is obviously very very difficult to beat the market, because there's so many shares out there that'll have you onto a loser. It gives me the indication that it's more of a sort of a game for the long term than the short term, with so many losing out, with the 85% not beating the market.

David:

Do you know what? In the wider industry, in the

professional fund management industry, these statistics are almost identical to what happens to fund managers. Out of all the funds that are available for people to buy, approximately 15% of professional fund managers will beat the market, and 85% of the fund managers will not beat the market. So do you find that quite frightening, that 85% of professionals do not beat the market?

Grant:

That is a surprise.

David:

That's a problem, isn't? So what's the point in stock picking, then?

As I forked over my vegetable plot, these words went around in my head. I then stopped and listened to it again. Had I heard it right – that virtually all professional fund managers, who are paid millions in bonuses each year, still couldn't beat the market? Surely that wasn't true.

Later that evening, lying in bed, the thought was still churning around in my head. Maybe my investment performance (or lack of it sometimes) over the last decade was not as unusual as I thought. My head buzzing, I got my iPhone out and started to Google.

I quickly found the answer to the question of whether only 15% of fund managers beat the market. Yes, it was true.

The reasons were not that complicated to understand, especially if you have a statistical mind. However, that search triggered even more questions. If this particular tenet of investing was not as I had been lead to believe, then what else would not stand up to critical appraisal with cold facts? As you'll see, quite a lot as it turns out. The rest is history and this book is a summary of what I discovered. The book was written in just over a month in January and February 2012, although much of the research was carried out in the latter part of 2011.

The structure of things to come

I have divided the book into two main sections.

- **The evidence.** The first section covers evidence on the returns that can be achieved from investing in shares. It compares these with the expectations of investors when they start and also with the theoretical projected returns published by the financial industry. It reveals that the average real-life private investor just doesn't make those returns because of three factors: lack of skill, the returns being lower than that of the index and, lastly, the effects of charges. Chapter 9 summarises the evidence and builds a model that quantifies exactly how much the average investor might be missing in their returns from all sources.
- **The implications.** Having established the facts, this section goes on to look at the consequences of these findings. It explores the implications for private investors overall, and particularly for their strategies. It

also assesses the implications for the finance industry and regulators.

In terms of how this book should be read, like most authors I'd love to think you'd sit down and read it from cover to cover. However, you could skim those chapters less relevant to you – if you do this, you'll find each chapter includes a summary of the key learning points to make this easier.

Is it for you?

I am writing the book for other private investors such as myself. My specific target is people who have been investing for a while and are reviewing their strategies. It is also relevant for those about to embark on investing in the stock market for the first time. I hope the latter group is not put off investing. That is not my intention.

However, given the wider implications of the findings, the book also has a second audience – namely, the finance industry itself and those that influence it (ie, regulators and the media). As you'll see, the findings should cause the industry to review its practices and particularly for how investing is sold to clients, to ensure they are more openly informed of the potential costs of investing, as well as the likely benefits.

If you're an academic, I've done my best to include references to pretty much every paper and article used so that you can read the sources yourself. If you're an economist, you may get frustrated at times because I don't go into as much mathematical detail as you probably think

I should. This is because I want the book to be fully comprehensible to my primary audience of ordinary investors.

Indeed, the latter group may think there are too many numbers in here as it is. However, the whole book is about how industry data are not quite as they may first seem, so they were included to show you why that is.

You will notice a strong UK bias. Indeed, I have quoted UK sources wherever possible. This is deliberate, as this book is targeted at UK investors and the figures on equity returns are all UK figures related to the FTSE. That is not to say the findings are not applicable to those living and investing in other markets. They are. If you are one of those people, I hope you will still read the book.

My life (and other animals)

To make it clear from the outset, I am just a private investor with an inquisitive mind. Since completing a psychology degree in 1981, I have worked as a market researcher most of my life and am still a director of a research agency I set up in 1998. I am not currently, nor ever have been, involved directly in the finance industry. I am not trying to sell you my magic system and I'm not in the pay of anybody in the industry who might gain by what I write, nor of any think tank trying to lobby for something.

I have been investing for over a decade and have learnt through bitter experience that some of my investments are successful and some are not – although, until recently, I did not know why. I have been far from a perfect investor in the past and have fallen into traps like everyone else. As evidence of this, I must admit to still holding my HMV shares (currently worth 2p as of January 2012) that I bought for 90p not long ago. However, I have had successes with my investments too, such as the great silver rally of spring 2011.

The animals? Two rabbits called Marley and Mimi who came in from the frozen garden quite often and nibbled at my feet when I was writing this book.

My sources are mixed – both spicy and piquant

During the writing this book, I have conversed with over 20 other private investors and asked for their thoughts. If you are one of those, can I thank you for your ideas and hopefully I've credited you in the correct places.

I have used the great resource that is the Internet to research a number of issues, and done my best to corroborate and seek source articles before presenting evidence. I am also indebted to the many investors and industry experts, and to columnists who regularly post financial articles, for both ideas and inspiration. The mainstream financial press such as the *Financial Times*, *Investors Chronicle* and *Moneyweek* have also all been incredibly useful sources of evidence.

If there is one area that I have not fully exploited in my research, it is that of all the thousands of published books on investing. Again, this was a deliberate policy, as I did not want my views to be influenced by the rose-tinted glasses of conventional wisdom. Instead, as a researcher, I wanted to look at issues afresh with a critical eye and review the original source evidence rather than just accepting the orthodoxy.

Given this, I am not claiming that what I have compiled here is a definitive collection of all the views and all the evidence. Where I'm missing key studies, I hope that readers will contact me or post comments on the book's website. My plan is to later update the book and include them.

I'm also indebted to...

I'll try and keep this short. First, I need to thank my wife and business partner Trish, who has not only put up with me while writing this book, but also significantly improved my manuscript is so many ways.

Then there are my beta readers whose comments have stopped me from dropping a few bloomers: Ray Poynter, Graeme Lawrence, Terry Odean and Alan Miller. Thanks also go to Laurie Donaldson for editing it so well.

There are also the many people who read version 1 and have mailed me with suggestions and errors. I hope I've included them all in this version. The rest will need to await v2!

I also have to thank Richard Crow, the inventor of the concept of a "monkey with a pin". Not only is he a successful private investor, he is also a graphic designer who created the cover for this book.

Why the title?

You may be struggling to work out why I called the book *Monkey with a Pin,* and are wondering what the link is between primates and investing. As you'll see in Chapter 3, monkeys can be as clever as the average investor, if not more so.

More specifically, "monkey with a pin" is an entrant in an annual share trading competition that randomly selects his stocks. In an average year, he manages to beat two thirds of all contestants. Last year, when I was researching the book, he was doing very well. Indeed, he finished the year in the top 10% of contestants. There is much investors can learn from this fact – hence the title.

The small print

I have tried to write as jargon-free as I can. Where I have used technical terms, I have tried to define them as I go along, rather than supply a glossary you have to keep turning to. One term that is worth mentioning here is *share* which, depending on context, I use interchangeably with the word *stock* (as they call them in the US) and *equities* (which the trade call them).

Also, on this subject, the book focuses heavily on shares (and funds that invest in them). It only briefly touches upon spread betting. It also gives little mention of other asset classes, such as bonds, property, commodities, etc.

I have done this to make the issues as simple and clear as possible for the reader. Investing in these other investments also has hidden costs and issues, although slightly different to share trading. However, these assets can be an important part of any investor's portfolio (as we'll see in Chapter 15).

Throughout the book you will read about *returns* and see percentages quoted. In most cases, these figures have allowed for the effects of inflation – that is, it has already been deducted so they show in real terms what something would be worth in today's money. With inflation so variable at the moment (and potentially increasing in the future), I have done this so that people can clearly see what the effects are.

I'm keen to hear your opinions on the book, so please post them at monkeywithapin.com. You can also download further free copies of the book from the website to distribute to your friends and colleagues.

Finally, to reiterate the disclaimer at the beginning of this book, the content is meant for informational and educational purposes only and it is not intended to be substitute for any legal, financial or other professional advice. Hopefully, in reading the book, you will understand more about investing and so make more money.

Enjoy the book.

@petecomley
pete.comley@monkeywithapin.com

1. http://www.fool.co.uk/news/investing/2011/05/03/transcript-lessons-from-a-schoolboy-investor.aspx accessed 18/1/2012.

Part I:
The Evidence

This section covers the evidence on what the returns are from investing in shares. It compares these with the expectations of investors when they start and also with the projected theoretical returns published by the financial industry.

It finds that the average real-life private investor just doesn't make those returns because of three factors: lack of skill, the returns of individual shares being lower than that of the index and finally the effects of charges.

Chapter 9 will then summarise the evidence and builds a model that quantifies exactly how much the average investor might be missing in their returns from all sources.

"I have only very recently started to invest in shares, essentially as a way of trying to increase my savings as the interest rate is so poor on regular savings accounts, even ISAs."

Stephen, recent new investor

1

New Investor Expectations

This chapter looks at the expectations of new investors and particularly how those are framed by the investment industry and the Internet. For most people, the key goal is to achieve significantly better returns than from a savings account.

The comment opposite, from one of the new investors I spoke to in my research, typifies why many people are starting to consider investing in the stock market. Because of the very low saving rates, there has been a marked shift in the profile of people trading for the first time in the UK. No longer is it largely the preserve of older retired men, it now appears to encompass a much broader and younger group of people seeking a return on their savings to try and beat inflation. Given this, the perspectives and expectations of a significant proportion of investors now tend to be somewhat different to what people have had in the past.

The long and winding road to investing

To fully understand these expectations, we need to first consider the process the average investor goes through. Some common themes emerge from the new investors that I spoke to. The first is that, for many, the road towards investing can be a long one. Although there are some who literally talked to a friend in the pub and came home and set up a trading account, these are the exceptions. Most people think about it for a long period, sometimes many years.

During that period, they are absorbing information about investing from reading articles in papers and magazines, talking with friends and, of course, trawling the World Wide Web.

In the UK, if you search the Internet for "investing in shares", you will find many useful articles – for example, those published on sites such as the Motley Fool.[1] You will also find adverts claiming to make you massive gains (eg, 85%) if you follow their system. However, unsurprisingly, the results are dominated by links to the biggest players in the online broking business. Their business is to encourage you to start investing – and particularly with them.

Most of them make the same argument, along the lines of:

- the stock market has historically outperformed cash savings;
- describing how much your £1,000 investment might have grown, over a carefully selected time period which shows tremendous growth; and, finally

- reminding you that if you keep your money in savings account at the moment, inflation will erode it.

All of the above statements contain some truth, as we'll see in the following chapters. However, it is the last point that the general public know to be true and that persuades many people to accept all three statements. Indeed, it is low savings rates versus inflation that has probably most caused the increase in client numbers for stockbrokers over the last few years.

Baggy trousers

A further factor that impacts on new investors' perceptions of returns is reading about successful traders. For example, many will have heard of the guru Antony Bolton, whose Fidelity Special Situations fund returned nearly 20% a year for nearly three decades. In addition, if one searches forums online, posts are full of those claiming to have made their fortune on shares. Many people claim to have achieved *10 baggers* (ie, increased their money 10 times on a share from, say, £1,000 to £10,000) or even the legendary *100 baggers*.

There are a few 100 baggers in the world, such as Merck & Co. (NYSE: MRK), which achieved it over a 30-year period. In the UK, about the best you might have done over recent times is Dominos Pizzas (DOM.L), which increased by around 30 times (briefly) in the period 2001–11. What these posts fail to present, though, is a true picture of how *all* investors fare, due to something called survivorship bias – a fact we'll discuss in more detail in Chapter 5.

5

Make millions – follow our system

These high levels of returns are also promoted in claims from those selling subscriber trading systems. Just put phrases like "becoming a millionaire investing in the stock market" into Google and you'll find them.

For example, ISACO is a UK company whose owner has recently written a book entitled *Liquid Millionaire – How to Make Millions from the Up and Coming Stock Market Boom*. Their website triumphs their aim "to help you return 12–15% per year over the long term". [2]

There are others that claim that if you invest your full ISA allowance each year (just over £10,000) for 15–20 years you could become a millionaire. Just follow their tips and system (for a fee).

Is it not surprising, therefore, when asking new investors what returns they expect, virtually all I spoke to expect over 5% and a substantial minority expect to make 25% or more per annum. As we'll see in the following chapters, these expectations are very wide of the mark in the current investment climate.

I suspect that if investors' expectations were more correctly anchored to their likely gains (bearing in mind the potential risks to capital), far fewer would embark on investing in the first place. This is a theme we shall return to later.

KEY LEARNING POINTS:

- Many now invest in the stock market because stockbrokers and other interested parties have told them they can get substantially better returns there than with savings accounts.
- This leads to expectations that their gains will be significant.

1. http://www.fool.co.uk/investing/guides/investing-terms-explained.aspx (accessed 18/1/2012).

2. http://www.isaco.co.uk/aboutus (accessed 23/2/2012).

"In the long term, stocks produce attractive returns. They may fluctuate in the short term ... but historically, they yield an investment return of about 10%."

Get Rich Slowly[1]

2

The Industry Evidence for Equity Returns

This chapter looks at the evidence of historical returns from the UK stock market. In particular, it focuses on the one study that is frequently used by the industry: The Barclays Equity Gilt Study.

Virtually all information published by the finance industry encouraging you to invest makes claims about projected returns from investing in the stock market in the long term. Like the example on the previous page, these are usually in absolute returns – ie, you will gain X% a year – although sometimes they are comparative, ie, how much more you would have gained versus just holding cash, the so-called "risk-free return".

The industry benchmark

If you look into the footnotes of these (UK) websites and publications, you will notice many point to the Barclays

Equity Gilt Study.[2] This is an annual publication issued by Barclays Capital which summarises data since 1899 on the returns on UK equities (ie, FTSE shares)[3] and "cash".[4]

Annual Real Returns on Equities and Cash (after inflation) 1899-2011

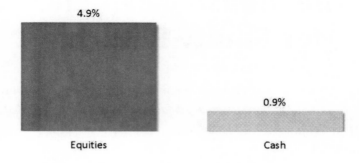

Based on data from: © "Barclays Equity Gilt Study 2012"

The latest published data covering the last 112 years[5] shows that equities have returned nearly 5% a year above that of the rate of inflation. In contrast, holding cash has beaten inflation by only around 1%.

Take care with that word "cash". Normally you'd expect it to mean the returns and interest you get from putting your money in a bank or building society account. However, as we'll see later, it is actually referring to the returns from something called Treasury bills, which are issued by the government.

The data is also split out into different time periods:

10

Annual Real Returns Over Different Time Periods (after inflation)

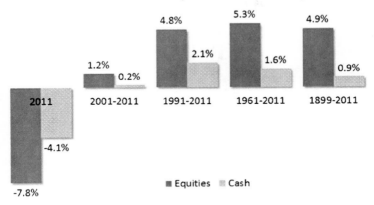

Based on data from: © "Barclays Equity Gilt Study 2012"

This shows that, over the last decade, returns from equities have been very low (1.2%) and hardly greater than cash (0.2%).

On the positive side, the Barclays Equity Gilt Study must be thanked for collating and extrapolating statistics on what the equity returns were before things like the FTSE All Share Index were created. It must also be commended for ensuring that the data it publishes properly take into account inflation.

In addition, their "real" return rates include the effects of reinvesting dividends. This means that, instead of looking at the returns just based on the value of the FTSE, they add an extra amount to it each year to allow for the dividend income.

Overall, the Barclays Equity Gilt Study has provided the finance industry for many decades with a common benchmark set of statistics that many in the industry refer to.

The Swiss give Barclays credit too

The Barclays data is supported by an alternative source of equity returns, now starting to be quoted in some reports from Elroy Dimson, Paul Marsh and Mike Staunton and being reprinted in the *Credit Suisse Global Investment Returns Sourcebook*.[6] Its authors' state, "we can be confident of the historical superiority of equities". Indeed, their data show very similar results for UK returns to Barclays:

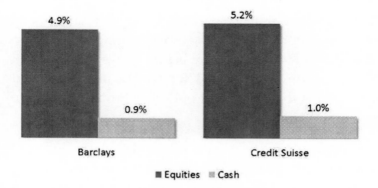

Annual Real Returns (after inflation)
1899-2011

Based on data from: © "Barclays Equity Gilt Study 2012" and © Elroy Dimson, Paul Marsh and Mike Staunton, *Credit Suisse Global Investment Returns Sourcebook 2012*

The slightly higher figures for Credit Suisse data are probably a reflection of their broader definition of the UK share market prior to the formation of the FTSE. However, the key point to note is that two sources, using different methods, give almost the same result – ie, about 5% real return per year on average.

In addition, the *Credit Suisse Sourcebook* also provides an international verification for these levels of returns, with the average return for the top 10 world stock markets over the last 112 years being very similar (ie, 4.7% worldwide versus 5.2% for the UK).

Top 10 World Stock Markets: Average Returns 1899-2011

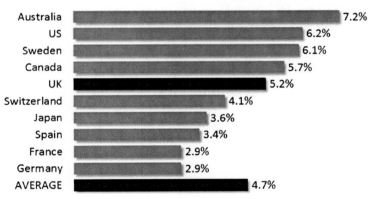

Based on data from: © Elroy Dimson, Paul Marsh and Mike Staunton, *Credit Suisse Global Investment Returns Sourcebook 2012*

Up, down, up, down, up, down, up, down

The Barclays report also publishes data for the increases in the equity index[7] without dividends for each year. Usefully, this is also provided adjusted for inflation, and I have presented it here with 1899 = 100.

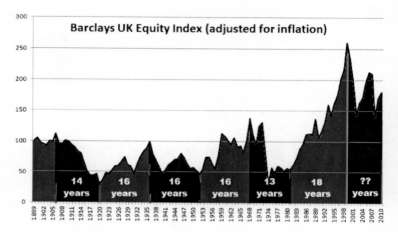

Based on data from: © "Barclays Equity Gilt Study 2012"

This data is quite interesting and not what I expected to see. First, it shows that for nearly 90 years (1900–1990), the UK share index had effectively gone nowhere at all, once you strip out inflation. This clearly demonstrates, over that period, the benefits of owning shares were driven mainly by the dividends and the compound interest on them (after you take out inflation).

The other fascinating aspect of the above chart is the cycles it illustrates. Not only do you see the normal business cycle of 5–8 years, which gives the picture a very jagged appearance, but it clearly exhibits a longer-term wave.

These so-called *secular* bull and bear market periods for the index typically last around 15–16 years each, with the total down/up cycle always lasting 30–32 years. In 2012, we are 12 years into a secular bear market that started in 2000.

There is an old adage, coined by Mark Twain, that "history never repeats itself, but it does rhyme". Given this, it is quite possible that the current secular bear market (red) on the FTSE will put in a new, possibly final, low at some point between now and 2014 before turning to a new secular bull market (ie, changes to upward and green). The implications of this will be discussed further in Chapter 13.

The *loads-a-money* era

The last clear fact from the chart is that the period from 1982 to 1999 was strange from a historical perspective. The size of the increases in the index during this period were unusual. For the first time since the previous century, the returns exceeded those created by just dividends and inflation. The average real growth per annum (including dividends) over that time was 13.2% pa. In contrast, for the whole period from 1899 to 1981, the average return was just 4% pa.

So what caused the unusual rise of equity assets in the 1980s and 1990s? My personal view is that a key reason goes back to August 15th 1971, when President Nixon unlinked the dollar peg from gold.[8] This heralded the start of an era of so-called *fiat currency*[9] in which it was possible for the finance industry to create infinite money – which they then used, among other things, to invest in shares.

The successful hedge fund manager Ray Dalio argues the rise seen during the 1980s and 1990s is a function of a much longer-term "debt cycle". It lasts approximately double the 32-year secular bull/bear cycle and can be between 50–75 years. It is his view this will mean that economy is likely to suffer a prolonged period of deleveraging over the next decade as this cycle is worked through.[10]

Another contributing factor for the rise in that period is related to demographics. The *New York Times* (January 5th 1998) wrote that "In the 1990s, the performance of the American stock market has been nothing short of amazing...Most of that performance has come from demographics, as the baby boom reaches the age when it seems wise to invest for retirement..." They also went on to predict that there would be an "asset meltdown" during the period when the baby boomers were selling their assets to pay for retirement – ie, now. Others[11] have argued the effects may not be as big as feared, but this will be another factor that will probably ensure that share prices do not revert to the rates of return seen in the 1980s and 1990s over the next few decades.

Is it really that simple?

Let's go back to the returns evidence. The claimed rate of return for equities since 1900 is around 5%. The data seem to back up the claim that investing in the UK stock market and holding those investments long-term, you are going to get much better performance than not only inflation but also holding cash over pretty much any long period.

They key problem with all this data is that it is too simplistic. It is also just a *theoretical* value. There are, in fact, three key elements[12] that will impact the real investor's returns from shares that have not been fully included:

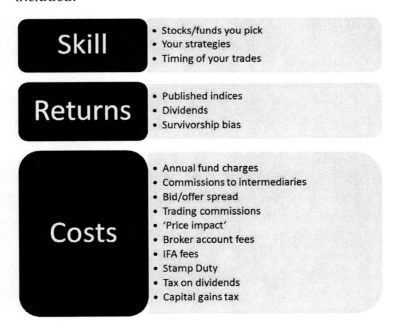

The next few sections will therefore look at all these factors in more detail and attempt to quantify exactly how important each of them is and what effect they have on the returns of the average investor. In Chapter 9, we'll then review the industry figures again and attempt to calculate a return from investing in the stock market versus holding cash for a real investor.

KEY LEARNING POINTS:

- The industry claimed average return on shares over the last 112 years is about 5%, after taking into account inflation and reinvesting of dividends.
- The industry data show that this significantly outperforms "cash", ie Treasury bills.
- This data is based on "theoretical" returns and ignores many factors that will affect the returns of the average investor (particularly costs).
- The market appears to exhibit pronounced cycles – a short-term business cycle of 5–8 years, a secular trend of around 32 years and a debt cycle of approximately double that.
- The massive growth of the stock market during the 1980s and 1990s was unusual from a historical perspective. This was probably a result of the creation of infinite money supply by removing the gold standard, although demographics may also have played their part.

1. http://www.getrichslowly.org/blog/2008/12/16/how-much-does-the-stock-market-actually-return/ (accessed 19/01/2012).

2. The full 2011 edition can be found here: http://www.stockbrokers.barclays.co.uk/content/research/reports/specialreports/documents/Barclays%20Equity%20Gilt%20Study%202011~2011-02-18%2013_29.pdf (accessed 20/1/2012). There is currently no public access to the 2012 edition.

3. More precisely, the equity returns between 1899 and 1935 are calculated from a "new Equity Index", consisting of the 30 largest shares by market capitalisation in each year; between 1935 and 1962 they are calculated

from the FT 30 index, and from 1962 onwards they are derived from the FTSE Actuaries All-Share Index.

4. More recently, they have also added index-linked gilts and corporate bonds to the comparison charts. They also started collecting returns from building society accounts in 1945, but they do not include these in the key comparison charts (they are only available in the Appendix).

5.http://uk.finance.yahoo.com/news/bonds-beat-shares-over-20-153000060.html (accessed 19/2/2012).

6. © Elroy Dimson, Paul Marsh and Mike Staunton, *Credit Suisse Global Investment Returns Sourcebook 2012* (see https://infocus.credit-suisse.com/app/_customtags/download_tracker.cfm?dom=infocus.credit-suisse.com&doc=/data/_product_documents/_shop/300847/credit_suisse _global_investment_yearbook_2011.pdf&ts=20110326172226, accessed 25/1/2012). Also, Elroy Dimson, Paul Marsh and Mike Staunton, *Triumph of the Optimists: 101 Years of Global Investment Returns* (Princeton, NJ: Princeton University Press, 2002).

7. These figures and those in the graph are effectively the equivalent of the FTSE All Share Index adjusted for inflation. Unlike the total returns quoted in the previous tables, this excludes dividends and their compounding effect. However, it does allow you to clearly see the growth effect of the index over time.

8. David Grabber, *Debt: The First 5,000 Years* (Brooklyn, NY: Melville House Publishing, 2011).

9. http://en.wikipedia.org/wiki/Fiat_money (accessed 25/1/2012).

10.http://www.bwater.com/Uploads/FileManager/research/how-the-economic-machine-works/a-template-for-understanding--ray-dalio-bridgewater.pdf (accessed 12/3/2012).

11. Kyung-Mook Lim and David N. Weil, 2003, "The Baby Boom and the Stock Market Boom" (see http://www.brown.edu/Departments/Economics/Papers/2003/2003-7_paper.pdf, accessed 25/1/2012).

12. For the mathematically minded, this can be summarised as: Returns = $\alpha + \beta - \gamma$, where α = skill, β = returns and γ = costs.

"*It's a fact of investment life that around 80% of all actively managed funds undershoot the stock market average over the long term. Given that most professional fund managers, with all their research, industry contacts and experience, can't consistently beat the stock market, what chance is there for the novice Fool? Don't believe that just because the professionals fail, the amateur stands a better chance. It just isn't the case.*"

The Motley Fool[1]

3

Skill – The Evidence from Competitions

In the previous chapter we saw that there were three factors that affect real investors' returns. We now look at trying to determine how much above (or below) the market the average private investor performs. There are two chapters on this subject. This first one focuses on the results of investing competitions.

The quote on the previous page comes from one of the investing guides published by The Motley Fool. It was also the root of the comment by David Kuo in his podcast that got me writing this book in the first place.

Searching for the holy grail

So as I lay in bed that evening back in May 2011, chewing this issue over, I thought: where can I find the evidence to back up this statement? My first obvious thought was that the stockbroking firms must know this and be able to tell me exactly how much their customers gain or lose from the market over a period of time (which I can then compare with how the market performs).

I therefore asked one of the biggest stockbroking firms in the UK for the answer. They took my request seriously and replied to me quite honestly (to my knowledge). They just did not know. Moreover, they said to carry out such a calculation would actually be extremely complicated because of trying to tie up all the buys and sells, etc.[2] Therefore, they had not attempted to do it.

Back to the competitions then...

So having drawn a blank there, my next thought was to look at competition evidence. There are actually quite a number of UK investing competitions. Some are run to encourage people to invest with a particular company or its funds (eg, Barclays Fantasy Investment Game),[3] while others seems to be genuinely more independently run (eg, GATS Investing Competition).[4]

They were not my first choice for this type of data, as you can always argue that those taking part may not be representative of the investing universe. In addition, some involve fantasy portfolios (without real money) so it could be claimed that participants might be more likely to pick riskier stocks than they might do with their own money.

However, balanced against this, the people taking part do appear to take them very seriously and spend a lot of time researching and justifying their choices. This is illustrated later on in that David Kuo podcast and on the posts on forums related to the competitions. Moreover, there is a lot of kudos involved in winning or performing well.

They are also very public competitions. Excepting the schools ones, I'd argue that they probably only attract participants who are both experienced and genuinely think they are above average in their investing prowess. If anything, then, the bias for most of these competitions will be towards those with a higher alpha (or skill level).

Can kids beat the finance industry?

However, let's start with looking at the results of the Shares4School competition run by The Share Centre.[5] This is held among A level students where 50–100 schools and colleges battle it out to see who can make the most money between October and May each year. What distinguishes this competition from some other similar ones is that participants are using real money, as they have to raise £1,500 to enter. There are other rules, including that the requirement to undertake at least one transaction per month and also a more recent rule that they can't have more than 50% of their portfolio in cash.

What I find interesting about this competition is that it is probably a very good surrogate for what people achieve in the first months of investing. You could argue that these students probably do better than the average person, because they have to discuss and argue for what they invest in as part of a group. They are also usually tutored by economics teachers – although, given the old adage about no two economists ever agreeing, some may argue that could be a negative!

So, what are the results?[6] The latest full year of the competition ended in May 2011. Grant, the boy in the David Kuo interview, came from Liverpool Bluecoat School. They ended up the year with £1,392 ie, a loss of –7.2% over seven months, but still a better result than many. Indeed, the average school lost –13.1%. Over the same period, the FTSE All Share Index gained +6.1% and, if you allow for dividends, showed a net return of +8.1%.[7]

Just six of the 72 schools taking part managed to beat the FTSE. The average difference versus the theoretical FTSE in seven months was –21.2% (ie, more than one fifth of their portfolio value). That represents a lot of real cash that the schools had invested and lost over the seven months.

Results of Shares4Schools Competition 2011

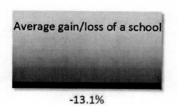

8.1%

Average gain/loss of a school

FTSE All Share Index gain/loss

-13.1%

Based on data from: Shares4Schools and author calculations

In case you think this was a one-off, the results of the 2011–12 competition (at the time of writing, mid competition) show a similar pattern although less extreme results (ie, FTSE up 9%, with the average school performance being 0%).

Take the challenge

One of the longest running of the UK independent competitions is Stock Challenge.[8] It has been running both annual and monthly competitions since 2003–4. Their annual competitions attract hundreds of investors competing for not only the fame of beating their colleagues, but also a prize. It is a fantasy portfolio competition and does not involve real money. However, it does mimic well the *buy and hold* strategy many investors adopt (see Chapter 13 for more on this). Participants are asked to pick five different stocks listed on the London Stock Exchange at the beginning of the competition (January 1st) and the winner is the one with the highest portfolio value, including dividends, at the end of the year (December 31st).

Although they run monthly competitions, I have focused my attention on the annual ones, as investing is long term (and, arguably, they should look at the results over a longer period than this). The following chart shows the results of the annual competitions since 2004.[9] I have worked out the net gain/loss of the average investor each year. For example, in 2011 the average investor lost −35.4% in the competition, while the FTSE All Share Index only declined −4.9%,[10] making a net loss versus the market of −30.5%.

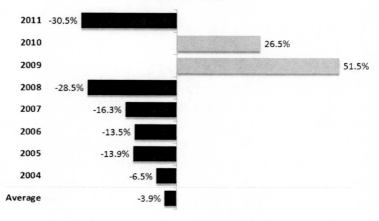

% Net Gain/Loss of UK StockChallenge Investors vs FTSE

2011	-30.5%
2010	26.5%
2009	51.5%
2008	-28.5%
2007	-16.3%
2006	-13.5%
2005	-13.9%
2004	-6.5%
Average	-3.9%

Based on data from: UKStockChallenge and author calculations

On average, experienced investors' underperformance was about 4% across all years. As can be seen, only in two of the eight years did they actually beat the FTSE. In addition, around 70% of competitors failed to beat the FTSE across all the years. This is quite a staggering level of underperformance – although not as high as that quoted by The Motley Fool at the beginning of this chapter, for reasons that will become apparent when we look at fees in Chapter 6.

Monkeys, pins and darts

If this was not bad enough, this competition also includes a computer-generated entry of five stocks on the London

Stock Exchange chosen at random. That random entry is called "Monkey with a Pin".[11] So, how does the monkey perform? Yes, you've guessed it, he can do rather well. In the most recent 2011 competition, Monkey with a Pin was in the top 10% of all investors. In an average year, the monkey normally beats nearly two thirds of experienced investors. How can this be? Is it just a freak result?

No, it is not. The apparent success of random stock picking is further verified by some analysis of the Investment Dartboard Competition run by the *Wall Street Journal (WSJ)*.[12] The *WSJ* ran 147 competitions between 1990 and 2002, where each month they pitted four top investment pros who picked one stock each, against the blindfolded editorial team who threw four darts into a copy of the stock listing in the paper.

Each monthly selection had its performance assessed at the end of the six-month competition. A quick analysis showed that the pros did slightly better, winning 61% of the time. However, there was a marked ramping effect caused by the pros' predictions, with the selected shares shooting up immediately on day 1 as the paper was published.

Given this, various academics have critiqued the competition saying that a fairer comparison of the returns of a real investor would be to take the stock prices at end of day 1 rather than the day before, as done by the *WSJ*. In addition to taking the stock prices on day 1, Gary Porter[13] of John Carroll University, re-examined the data in a way more akin to how the normal investor behaves.

He examined three scenarios with their stock picks. He first assumed that an investor was regularly saving a fixed amount every month of $4.[14] He then saved this in one of three ways, with these results:

Re-analysis of Wall Street Journal Random Darts vs Pro Investors Competition

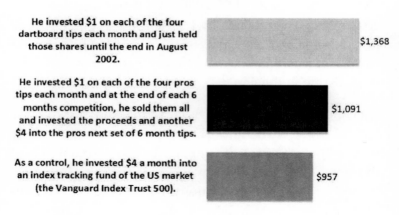

He invested $1 on each of the four dartboard tips each month and just held those shares until the end in August 2002. $1,368

He invested $1 on each of the four pros tips each month and at the end of each 6 months competition, he sold them all and invested the proceeds and another $4 into the pros next set of 6 month tips. $1,091

As a control, he invested $4 a month into an index tracking fund of the US market (the Vanguard Index Trust 500). $957

Based on data from: E. Porter (2004)

The results were staggering. Not only did a simple buy and hold strategy using the dartboard stocks beat a strategy that always followed the latest tips from the pros, it also beat a simple buy and hold index-tracking strategy.

Even more clever monkeys

Since releasing the first edition of this book a number of readers have told me about other *monkey* experiments - all of which show the same results.

The *IFS Student Investor Challenge*[17] also has a Monkey entry which buys and holds 10 stocks at random. In the latest competition which ended in February 2012, he was ranked 1223 out of 7366 contestants, ie in the top sixth of all the players.

The one I like the best though is about Ola the Chimp[18] .In 1993, the Swedish newspaper *Expressen* trained him to throw real darts into the newspaper. They then gave him $1250 and a set of darts and pitted him against five professional traders for a month. Needless to say, Ola won the competition with four times the gains of the best pro.

However there are many more. For example, in the mid noughties, the *Chicago Sun-Times* employed a monkey called Mr Monk[19] to manage a portfolio over a number of years. He picked stocks by marking them with a red pen in the paper. In all but one year from 2003-2008 he beat the market. He also beat the expert stock picker Jim Cramer most years.

More recently in 2010, a Russian monkey called Lusha[20] picked stocks by using building blocks with their names on. Over a period of one year, her portfolio grew three times in value, beating 94% of Russian professional fund managers.

So, again, I ask how can it be that monkeys are such good stock traders?

Why the monkeys are so smart

Perhaps part of the answer lies with Princeton University economics professor Burton Malkiel. It was he who quipped in his 1973 book, *A Random Walk Down Wall Street*, about blindfolded monkeys throwing darts being as good at stock picking as the professionals – which inspired so many of these competitions. He believed in what is called the *efficient market hypothesis*[15] (EMH), that argues that all available information is quickly factored into stock prices so that all stocks present equal chances for gains.

But this still does not explain why the monkeys keep beating the index. Surely the EMH would suggest that they should just mirror it? For that you need to understand some of the flaws in the EMH. Don't get me wrong, the EMH does indeed explain most stock movements, but not all, so let's look at some of the problems with it.

Firstly the market does not always correctly value smaller companies where less information is available or verifiable. Therefore a monkey with his random stock picking may be more likely to include these in his portfolio.

Indeed the benchmark indices are weighted towards the larger companies – for example, currently 50% of the change in the FTSE 100 is accounted for by only 10 shares. These are mature companies that, by definition, are also probably companies that are slower growing than a random selection of the index (see discussion on this in Chapter 5).

Indeed, there is real evidence[16] that you are better to have a portfolio that is equally weighted across all its stocks than one that is value weighted towards holding more of the larger ones (which show this negative bias). Again monkeys will do this naturally.

Against the EMH theory, there is clear evidence that the market over-reacts emotionally to both fear and greed and excessive volatility can occur in share prices - particularly in market crashes. The monkey's lack of appreciation of these helps him particularly avoid panicking and selling prematurely at a loss. Furthermore the monkey's innate ability to ignore the media and not get suckered into stories also helps - see Chapter 12.

Finally on emotions, unlike the monkeys, the experts probably pick slightly riskier stocks in competitions, as they know that to win; they've got to take some chances. This means that their gains may be higher in some circumstances, but on average their losses are probably greater.

Returning to the key question

So where does this all lead us in determining what is the impact of the average stock-picking skill on investor performance? The answer looks negative. In the next chapter we'll review some more detailed studies of investor performance based on analysis of real trading records and try to put some precise figures on it.

A true story

First, however, I thought I'd share the story of a new investor, six months into their trading life – which was written in February 2010, a period when investing should have been fairly easy, as the FTSE rose by nearly 25%. I think it confirms the view that trading is a difficult skill to acquire for most of us.

"I am 26 years old and started to trade in the summer of 2009. Realising the fact that my savings were being depreciated year upon year, I decided to invest in the stock market. This is my trading experience to date.

Just three days after deciding to invest in the stock market, I was holding shares in a few companies. This was my first mistake, rushing into the stock market and trying to make money quickly.

I would also recommend anyone contemplating share trading to set up a "dummy" share dealing account, where potential investors can try share dealing without actually losing any money. If I had done this, I would have saved a lot of money.

Within the first few months, my portfolio was down and I was selling shares at losses. One of the principal lessons I have learnt is that it is very easy to lose money on the stock market without research. Making money in the stock market is not easy and, without research, I would say it is incredibly difficult. During the first months of my trading, I spent no time on research and chased many stocks from the "top risers" list and from tips from the bulletin boards, hoping for quick gains. I am still paying for some of these mistakes, as I am "locked" into many shares. Some of these "quick gains" are currently down 30% in my portfolio. I have learnt not to trust everyone on the bulletin boards and learnt that not everything posted on these boards is entirely true.

Watching my portfolio depreciate day by day was very difficult for me. I was always trying to recover my losses and taking wild punts into the "risky/high reward" category. Some of my other mistakes included buying a share on a RNS [news bulletin announcement], not realising the well-known phrase "buy on speculation, sell on news".

Emotions can play a key part in buying and selling. I still have to master this aspect of trading. Controlling these emotions to ensure they don't cloud your judgement in buying or selling is a key aspect of trading.

I am learning the hard way, but in some strange way am glad to have made the mistakes this early in my journey. Thankfully for me, I have met some great people via the bulletin boards who have helped me a great deal. I have been given support, advice and guidance which have helped me increase my knowledge in share trading. I have witnessed some shocking behaviour on bulletin boards with people attempting to drive prices up or down with lies and false information.

For the past few months, I have been in the process of restructuring my portfolio by reducing, or at times replacing, some of my losers with companies where I see future growth and potential. It will be one year this summer 2010 when I started my journey, and I am confident I will be able to turn my portfolio around. I believe in learning from my mistakes and acquiring more knowledge will enable me to become a successful investor."

Iqbal, private investor

POSTSCRIPT ADDED TWO YEARS LATER:

"Reviewing my experience in the spring of 2012, almost three years since I started trading, I have definitely become a wiser investor; note the use of the word investor rather than a trader. The markets in general have a difficult time with the euro zone debt problems and most companies on the stock exchange have suffered as a result.

My current portfolio is down 35% (without adding in the effects of inflation), some of the mistakes made when I initially started are still sitting in my portfolio. My advice to anyone thinking of starting in this game is to understand the stock market and only "play" with money you can afford to lose. This is not an easy game, there is no such thing as easy money."

KEY LEARNING POINTS:

- New investors (like those in the school competitions) could be losing significant amounts of money in their initial trades.
- Even more experienced private investors in competitions still perform worse than the market on average.

- Monkeys can beat the average human investor, ie, random stock picking might be a more successful strategy than selecting them.
- Monkeys might be doing better because of the efficient market hypothesis, ie, everything that is known about a stock is already priced into it, so any stock is as likely to be a future winner as any other. It might also be partly related to average better performance of smaller than larger stocks in some way.

1. http://www.fool.co.uk/Investing/guides/Can-You-Beat-The-Market.aspx (accessed 24/01/2012).

2. As I later discovered (see the next chapter), some people in the US have successfully done this analysis on brokers' records.

3. https://www.barclaysfantasyfundmanager.co.uk/ (accessed 25/1/2012).

4. http://boards.fool.co.uk/gats-investing-contest-51685.aspx?mid=12239690 (accessed 25/1/2012).

5. http://www.shares4schools.org/ (accessed 25/1/2012).

6. http://www.shares4schools.org/league-national.html (accessed 23/6/2011). Note the 2010/11 results have now been overwritten by the latest competition.

7. Assuming an annual 3.5% dividend for seven months.

8. http://www.stockchallenge.co.uk/ (accessed 25/1/2012).

9. 2003 was the first competition, but it had less than a hundred competitors and lacked "monkey with a pin".

10. Dividends assumed to be 3.5% pa.

11. Originally suggested by one of the entrants called Cockney Rebel (aka Richard Crow in real life). He commented to the competition organisers that "a monkey with a bleedin' pin could do better" than him and the other contestants most of the time. They then started including it in their 2004 competition onward. Indeed, in its first competition, it beat 60% of the entrants (ie, better than chance) and also the FTSE 100! Richard Crow is a regular investor and one of the few who does seem to have a positive alpha. He is also a graphic designer and created the front cover for this book.

12. http://www.investorhome.com/darts.htm (accessed 25/1/2012).

13. Gary E. Porter, 2004, "The Long-term Value of Analysts' Advice in the Wall Street Journal's Investment Dartboard Contest", *Journal of Applied Finance*, 14(2), Fall/Winter.

14. He also included typical trading costs of 0.5% per trade in his calculation.

15. http://en.wikipedia.org/wiki/Efficient-market_hypothesis (accessed 25/1/2012).

16. Yuliya Plyakha, Raman Uppal and Grigory Vilko, 2012, "Why Does an Equal-weighted Portfolio Outperform Value- and Price-weighted Portfolios?", EDHEC Business School, March.

17. http://www.studentinvestor.org. (accessed 10/5/2012).

18. James Dunn, *Share Investing for Dummies* (John Wiley & Sons Australia Ltd, 2007).

19. http://www.freeby50.com/2009/04/jim-cramer-versus-monkey-who-wins.html. (accessed 10/5/2012).

20. http://www.dailymail.co.uk/news/article-1242575/Lusha-monkey-outperforms-94-Russia-bankers-investment-portfolio.html (accessed 10/5/2012).

"Our empirical analysis presents a remarkably clear portrait of who gains from trading: individuals lose, institutions win."

Brad Barber *et al*,[1]

4

Skill – The Real Numbers

This chapter focuses on the published literature with the aim of determining how much above (or below) the market the average investor performs. It then attempts to quantify this number exactly by drawing the data from this and the previous chapter together.

WARNING: This chapter contains lots of numbers. Bear with them. It is important to understand these studies and what they show.

I almost called this section "estimating skill revisited". Roll forward nine months from when I did the initial research on the competitions after listening to David Kuo's podcast. I have decided I am definitely going to write this book. The pressures of my day job as a market researcher have lessened, so I have some time to carry out a thorough investigation of the published academic literature on investor performance.

Given the comment from that UK stockbroker that they had no idea what the returns of their customers were and that such calculations were almost impossible, I did not expect to discover much. However, I was surprised to find a number of studies had been conducted over the last few decades on the subject, including one which analysed every single transaction record on an exchange over a five-year period (more on this anon).

Hot hands

Before looking at these, it is worth briefly considering the reasons why an investor might have a high or low skill level (or *alpha*). In the literature, there is frequent reference to a concept called "hot hands". This has nothing to do with anxious perspiring investors with weak handshakes, but is a basketball term to describe someone on a winning streak able to hit a number of successful shots in a row.[2]

Many have argued, and indeed there is evidence, that some people are genuinely good at investing. This is probably partly related to inherited temperament and partly from learnt behaviour (see Chapter 12 for the proof and a more detailed discussion on this topic). Think famous investors such as Warren Buffett and possibly people like Jesse Livermore,[3] although even the latter did lose his whole fortune a few times along the way.

However, it appears that these people are very few and far between and your chances of having consistently "hot hands" are extremely low. Indeed, Hal Heaton of Brigham Young University[4] reckons that just 5% of investors (including pros) can beat the market over five years and that 0.1% beat it over 10 years – a result he notes as being similar to chance.

The results for professional fund managers are arguably even worse. Lipper[5] published a report called "Beating the Benchmark" in March 2012, which looked at how all European active fund managers performed versus their respective benchmark (before fees). Only 43% of them could beat their index in an average year.

Indeed, over the last three years (2009–11), only 8.6% of funds consistently beat their benchmark index. For the mathematically minded, this is much worse than random chance, which would have predicted that 12.5% could beat their index.

Random noise (almost)

Therefore, with my statistician's hat on, I believe you can look at the distribution of investors as follows:

Distribution of investor returns

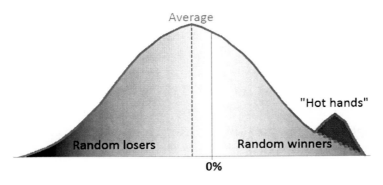

Source: monkeywithapin.com

Most investors' returns probably follow a normal random distribution. There is, however, a group who do manage to beat the system (the "hot hands", or whatever you want to call them). These include many professional city traders and some private investors. We'll discuss in more detail what actually distinguishes them in Chapter 12; however, their existence does mean that the average return for a private investor (dotted blue line in the above graph) is below zero.

Personally, I think the success of the monkeys at investing clearly shows that a lot of the returns we achieve are down to mere random chance. But what are the main factors that drag down your alpha/skill below the apes? There are two main ones:

- *What shares/funds you pick* – and we'll talk in detail about problems with investment strategies in Chapter 13.
- *Your timing* – especially with many private investors buying too high and selling too low (see Chapter 12).

Crowds don't always have wisdom

One of the most interesting recent papers evaluates the effectiveness of a website which collects real investors' stock predictions in the US. It is called CAPS (http://caps.fool.com). Contrary to the efficient market hypothesis (see previous chapter), it attempts to capture investor sentiment and prove that the "wisdom of the crowd"[6] can correctly pick stocks. It now has over 170,000 investors rating over 5,000 US stocks every year. Arguably, it offers a potentially good sample of investors and their stock picking opinions and decisions.

Christopher Avery *et al*[7] reviewed the 2.5 million predictions made on the website between November 2006 and December 2008. Despite a press release proclaiming this study vindicated the success of the system, an examination of the actual paper reveals a somewhat different story. Five out of six of the predictions made by the 60,000+ investors were "buy" predictions. Of these, the average value declined over the following six-month period versus the market by –1.1%.

However, on a positive note for CAPS, it did appear to more accurately predict when to sell stocks[8] – these declined by 5.3% versus the market. Unfortunately, I suspect more people are interested in using the CAPS ratings to decide what to buy, than what/when to sell, so this predictive power may well be wasted. Moreover, in helping us define what returns someone will get from buying a stock, they are by definition irrelevant (all that they tell you are how much more you would have lost if you did not sell up).

Another issue with this study is *survivorship bias* (a concept we're go into in more detail in the next chapter). Those stock picks performing so badly that they became delisted or were too small were excluded from the analysis. The authors claim these represent 0.4% of the sample, and arguably this amount also ought to be added to the net loss suffered by people trading the "buy" predictions of –1.1%.

Terry's dissertation

So, let's return to my original quest to see what happens when you analyse real investors' returns. One for the first papers to be written on this was by Terry Odean, as part of his dissertation at the University of California, Berkeley in 1996, and later published as a journal article.[9] He examined the records of nearly 100,000 trades with a discount broker between 1987 and 1993. He found that, on average, the stocks people bought declined by 2.7% over the following year and the ones they sold increased by 0.5%. This implies that their market timing may not be very good, but it does not tell us much about the actual returns of investors.

However, he did note that over a half of the clients closed their accounts within seven years and over a quarter closed their account within one year. He did not show the results separately by these groups unfortunately, but one can only speculate that those closing their accounts probably included those with the greatest losses.

Terry then went on to work further on similar data with Brad Barber[10] (also of Berkeley), presenting a paper provocatively entitled: "Trading Is Hazardous to Your Wealth". They analysed over 66,000 accounts of stock traders with a discount broker between 1991 and 1996.

They found that the average investor lost –1.5% per annum after inflation. However, their losses were primarily driven by commission charges. Indeed, without these, investors would have made a slight gain versus the market and inflation of 0.9% per annum, implying that alpha may be slightly positive for these real investors during this time period of investing conditions.

However, it should be noted that this data was from a period that saw abnormally consistent positive returns on the stock market and this could have had an influence on the results – ie, the smaller, riskier stocks in which this group were more frequently investing being more profitable than the index.

Their paper also went on to analyse the results of the subset of frequent traders. Unsurprisingly, this group loses more (–6.5%) because they have more charges to pay. The authors conclude that these people are trading too much because of overconfidence in their abilities.

A billion trades later

Another key paper[11] was written by a duo who, in collaboration with some Taiwanese colleagues, managed to get permission to analyse *all* of the trading records on the Taiwan stock exchange between 1995 and 1999 – over 1 billion trades. This information not only allowed them to look at the success (or not) of real trades but to examine whether people were private investors or pros in the finance world.

The period for which the data was taken covers both a bull market and the Asian Crisis bear market, making it a good analogue for the current state of markets in places like the UK. There are, however, some differences worth mentioning about Taiwan before we look at the results in detail. First, at that time Taiwan had a lot of day traders, so across their whole dataset there are probably three times as many trades as you'd currently expect in somewhere like the UK. Trading costs are also much lower there with commissions capped at 0.14% per trade, with just 0.3% stamp duty on sales. Just over a half of the shares in Taiwan are owned by private investors, much higher than the UK (where it is only around 10%). The proportion of the population who frequently trade shares is also higher.

So what were the results? They are very clear. The *average Taiwanese private investor lost net 3.8% per year* after allowing for changes in the underlying market index. The table below shows how this can be broken down due to different factors:

Amounts Lost Per Year by the Average Taiwanese Investor

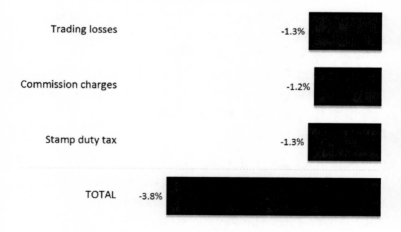

Based on data from: Barber *et al* (2005) and author calculations

Is it a zero sum game?

What is also interesting is that investing has to be zero sum game[12] versus the index. In other words, if you have beaten the index, someone else must have done worse than it. What Brad, Terry and their colleagues were able to prove was that private investors' trading losses due to poor skill went entirely to the professional institutional investors. They suggest that Taiwanese professionals gain 1.5%[13] pa above the market at the expense of the 1.3% losses by private investors.

Note, though, that these numbers for professional gains will not directly translate across to the UK or the US, because private investors represent less than 10% of trades in these countries (as opposed to nearly 60% in Taiwan). Assuming private investors lose –1.3%, this equates to an alpha for professionals in the UK/US of just +0.2% – ie, barely above zero.

This is backed up by evidence that compares how many fund managers consistently get in the top rankings over many years. The answer is very few and hardly above the level of random chance.[14]

Why the pros do better

More recently, there has been further discussion of exactly how some professionals manage to outperform private investors. Tim Richards, who posts the Psy–Fi blog, thinks the pros are always one step ahead. [15] For example, they are using factors such *high-frequency trading* (ie, using computer algorithms to trade and hold positions for

47

fractions of seconds), the introduction of *dark pools* (ie, trading platforms which circumvent the normal stock exchanges) and, most recently, the use of automated analysis of social media trends. According to Richards, this combination "gives wealthy institutions skewed and privileged access to the data needed to make informed trading choices".

Another possibility is that the size of purchases made by some influential professional investors can shape the market. By definition, they get in earlier on trends (as they create them), leaving private investors to join them later and at a point when there are fewer potential profits and more potential downside.

For example, think when Warren Buffett invests. Not only does he normally do so when the price of a stock is low, he normally gets a good deal on it. However, by the time the private investor buys, a lot of the price action has already taken place. A similar thing happened with the tips from the pros in the *WSJ* noted in the previous chapter. The main increase took place before the private investor had a chance to buy.

Hard times for US fund investors

All of the above data deal with share trading. So, what evidence is there for people who invest in funds, like mutual funds in the US or unit trusts in the UK?

One of the most frequently quoted studies is DALBAR's "Qualitative Analysis of Investor Behavior (QAIB)".[16] This takes data from the Investment Company Institute covering all US mutual funds. It then looks at inflows and outflows of capital for each fund to deduce the real returns of investors overall in such products.

The results for the last 20 years are quite disappointing for any fund investor. They show that returns after inflation over the last 20 years for the average investor were losses of just over 5%pa[17] compared with the return on the S&P index.

The authors put the majority of blame down to psychological factors in investors, and particularly their bad timing. Charges also make up a part of the difference, although the two are not distinguished in the reporting. However, it is likely that charges amount to maybe –2%. Therefore, the poor skill element will be around –3.3% pa.

To give you an idea of the size of the problem with market timing, take a look at some UK data published by the Investment Management Association (IMA) on net inflows into UK funds. The chart clearly shows that inflows peak when the FTSE reaches its top, and outflows are at their highest when it drops. This demonstrates how much people's investing is influenced by media headlines of share prices rocketing or plummeting. However, from an investing point of view, buying at the top of the market is clearly going to impact on your potential returns.

Fund Sales are Correlated to the FTSE

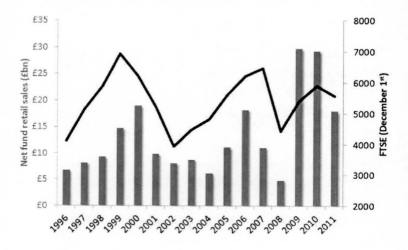

Based on data from: IMA

As further evidence of this, Morningstar also report real investor returns in their data on funds. [18] In a 2010 article, they presented findings that the average gap they had calculated between theoretical returns and actual returns was –2.8% over the last 15 years. This is not as high as the DALBAR figure, a difference probably explained by them only covering 15 years. The Morningstar data do not appear to include charges either.

An earlier study revealed a slightly lower figure still. Geoffrey Friesen and Travis Sapp analysed US mutual funds between 1991 and 2004, calculating a figure of –1.6% pa performance gap due to the bad timing of trading. [19]

Brits not much better either

So what does the data show for UK unit trusts and funds? A recent paper from Andrew Clare and Nick Motson of CASS Business School in London analysed 1,362 funds covered by the IMA in the UK between 1992 and 2009. They found a performance gap of –1.2% pa due to the bad timing of investments, slightly lower than that observed in the US work.

Note though this study, like others on funds, probably does not fully take into account something called survivorship bias – ie, does not factor in the effects of funds that merge or are suspended. This will result in actual returns being worse (see the next chapter, which focuses entirely on quantifying this issue).

Putting the jigsaw pieces together

So let's try and draw this all together to work out an estimate for skill (or alpha) – ie, how much extra does a private investor make/lose compared with the market before charges are taken into account. There looks as if there is a clear correlation between knowledge/experience and skill. Those who are new to investing (like the students in the competition) suffer higher losses, as do those who are less engaged/knowledgeable (eg, fund investors). The most experienced (ie, industry professionals) are the only group who have a slight positive alpha.

- For fund investors, the average of the four studies quoted above (excluding charges) is –2.2%.

- For stock investors, the best estimate is probably that from the Taiwan study, ie, −1.3%.

The latter estimate ignores the slightly positive result of the Barber and Odean US study, but in their own words in the conclusion to the Taiwan study both admit the US study is less comprehensive (and, by implication, less reliable). The other reason to adopt a slight negative figure is all the other evidence from competitions and the like also point to losses for the average investor compared with the market.

KEY LEARNING POINTS:

- The average private investor's skill (or alpha) is negative meaning that, even without costs, they will normally underperform the market.
- Investors in funds underperform most. This is mainly as a result of poor timing, ie, investing most when the media highlight how well the market is doing and then selling when they see headlines of its decline.
- My best estimate of the actual values lost per year by poor skill alone is around −2.2% for fund investors and −1.3% for share investors.
- The average alpha for a UK fund manager is probably +0.2%.
- These estimates are largely based on an analysis of the actual results for investors of every one of the billion trades on the Taiwanese stock market in the late 1990s.

1. Brad M. Barber, Yi-Tsung Lee, Yu-Jane Li and Terrance Odean, 2005, University of California, Berkeley, working paper: http://finance.martinsewell.com/traders/Barber-etal2005.pdf (accessed 24/1/2012).

2. Interestingly, even in that field, detailed analysis of real records suggest there is not much evidence of players being able to do this any better than predicted by chance (see T. Gilovich, R. Vallone and A. Tversky, 1985, "The Hot Hand in Basketball: On the Misperception of Random Sequences", *Cognitive Psychology*, 17, pp 295–314.

3. http://en.wikipedia.org/wiki/Edwin_Lef%C3%A8vre (accessed 26/1/2012); also read his fascinating book *Reminiscences of a Stock Operator*, published in 1923.

4.http://www.deseretnews.com/article/640192882/Beating-market-is-tougher-than-it-seems.html (accessed 26/1/2012).

5.http://share.thomsonreuters.com/PR/Lipper/Reports/Lipper_Beating%20 the%20Benchmark_March2012.pdf (accessed 22/3/2012).

6. *The Wisdom of Crowds* is a book and a concept promoted by James Surowiecki, which argues that the aggregate of a large number of informed opinions should be better than any one individual (see http://en.wikipedia.org/wiki/The_Wisdom_of_Crowds (accessed 16/1/2012).

7. Christopher Avery, Judith A. Chevalier, Richard J. Zeckhauser, 2011, "The CAPS Prediction System and Stock Market Returns", NBER working paper no. 17298, August.

8. This CAPS analysis included a period of market turbulence and the great bear market decline at the end of 2008. Riskier stocks suffered more during that time than would be apparent from a value-weighted index. I personally think this may in part explain why negative predictions during this time were more accurate.

9. Terrance Odean, 1999, 1999, "Do Investors Trade Too Much?", *The American Economic Review*, 89(5), December, pp 1279–98.

10. Brad M. Barber and Terrance Odean, 2000, "Trading is Hazardous to Your Wealth: The Common Stock Investment Performance of Individual Investors", *The Journal of Finance*, 55(2), April, pp 773–806.

11. Brad M. Barber, Yi-Tsung Lee, Yu-Jane Li and Terrance Odean, 2005, "Who Loses from Trade?", evidence from Taiwan, University of California, Berkeley working paper.

12. The zero sum game is where one participant's losses are exactly matched by another's gains.

13. It is higher as they only represent 43% of the trades undertaken.

14.http://articles.businessinsider.com/2011-12-06/wall_street/30480448_1_fund-managers-bad-luck-john-paulson (accessed 28/3/2012).

15.http://www.psyfitec.com/2012/01/160-billion-dollar-bezzle.html (accessed 26/1/2012).

16. http://www.qaib.com/public/default.aspx (accessed 26/1/2012).

17. The actual figure was 5.3%, which is very similar to my estimates in section 9 when you add back in +1% for survivorship bias.

18. http://news.morningstar.com/articlenet/article.aspx?id=340334 (accessed 26/1/2012).

19. Geoffrey C. Friesen and Travis R. A. Sapp, 2007, "Mutual Fund Flows and Investor Returns: An Empirical Examination of Fund Investor Timing Ability", *Journal of Banking & Finance,* 31(9), pp 2796–816.

"During WWII, Allied bomber losses were high, so high that the British Air Ministry undertook a rigorous analysis in hopes of finding a solution. Their engineers set out to examine every bomber they could, gathering data on each bullet hole. After analysing the results, engineers decided to reinforce the areas that had the highest concentrations of holes with armour plating.

It didn't work.

Enter Abraham Wald, a mathematician, who suggested that they simply put extra armour plating where the bullet holes weren't. The idea was simple: if the planes are returning with bullet holes, obviously those areas can be struck without causing the planes to crash. The planes that weren't returning, Wald theorized, are the ones that are getting hit in different areas.

The engineers' error was so significant, statisticians decided to name it: survivorship bias."[1]

5

Returns – Is the Index Correct?

This chapter looks at how benchmark indices like the FTSE are calculated. It highlights a specific attribute that, over time, they will always rise, even though individual shares may not. This so-called survivorship bias has implications not only for equity return comparisons but also the likely long-term effectiveness of strategies such as buy and hold. Survivorship bias also affects fund performance statistics.

Long before I thought I'd write this book, I used to puzzle why the FTSE kept going up so relentlessly over the decades. I knew some of it must be to do with the fact that unsuccessful companies just disappeared, to be replaced by ones with a high rate of growth. However, I couldn't quite get my brain around what was going on and how this alchemy was performed. I know now...

What goes up doesn't have to come down

You first need to understand what major stock market indices are. Let's take the FTSE 100 as an example. It comprises the top 100 companies registered for trading in the UK as measured by their market capitalisation (calculated simply by multiplying the number of shares in circulation by their share price).

The index itself first began in January 1984 at a base value of 1000. Weights were created for each company in the index dependent on their size. This meant that movements in the larger companies would have more impact on the overall index. The index is calculated and republished continuously.

Every quarter, there is a reshuffle of the companies in the index. About three companies might typically leave and join each time – ie, you could potentially see 10 or more new companies join per year, but it is often less as some yo-yo in and out. At each reshuffle, they also alter the weighting to allow for changes in market capitalisation and also to include the new up-and-coming companies. However, they always ensure that the index starts a new quarter at the same number as it finished the previous one.

So, let's stop, recap and think about this. You have a system where you are perpetually measuring the increasing performance of the UK's fastest-growing companies only. Any company that has below-average performance will soon get relegated and stop dragging the index down and will be directly replaced by one that is growing.

The result: an ever-increasing index over a long period of time.

A decade of losers

Does this matter, you may ask, especially if you are investing in specific shares or a fund that may have just 10 shares in its portfolio. The answer is yes, because not only will it set wrong expectations for you regarding what happens to individual share prices, but it can also lead you to follow strategies like buy and hold, which may not perform quite as well as you expect.

Say 90% of the top companies in the FTSE 100 are going nowhere and their share price does not change over a year. The remaining 10% of companies are "dogs" and get relegated and are replaced by new entrants that increase in price over the year. These new companies will cause the FTSE to go up. But, hang on a minute, let's remember that 90% of the old index has not moved and the other 10% dropped in value (and got relegated) – yet the FTSE has gone up?

To illustrate this in practice, let's look at the top 20 constituents of FTSE a decade ago and see what has happened to them.

Change in the top 20 FTSE shares from 2001-2011

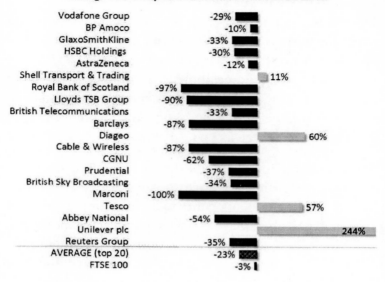

Vodafone Group	-29%
BP Amoco	-10%
GlaxoSmithKline	-33%
HSBC Holdings	-30%
AstraZeneca	-12%
Shell Transport & Trading	11%
Royal Bank of Scotland	-97%
Lloyds TSB Group	-90%
British Telecommunications	-33%
Barclays	-87%
Diageo	60%
Cable & Wireless	-87%
CGNU	-62%
Prudential	-37%
British Sky Broadcasting	-34%
Marconi	-100%
Tesco	57%
Abbey National	-54%
Unilever plc	244%
Reuters Group	-35%
AVERAGE (top 20)	-23%
FTSE 100	-3%

Source: monkeywithapin.com

Over the 10-year period from January 2001 to 2011, the published FTSE index barely moved (down −3%). In contrast, the average underperformance of these top 20 shares versus the index over this time period was −23%. Indeed, 16 of the 20 shares declined and one even went bust (Marconi). On an annual basis, the loss versus the index is equivalent to −1.8% pa if you'd followed a strategy of buying and holding the top 20 shares over this time period.

This is not a scientific measure of the true value of underperformance, as it just happens to be data for the last decade I had to hand when doing the analysis for this book. However, it does give you a feel for the effect this can have on investments in particular shares.

It's called survivorship bias

Having observed this phenomenon, I then discovered it is called survivorship bias, and that it affects not only indices, but also much of the research published by the finance industry and even many academic studies on stock effectiveness. It also affects most research you see published claiming that XYZ system would have made you a fortune had you followed it for the last 10 years.

This is because, despite an era of instantaneous stock prices, it is remarkably difficult to get hold of good historical records for companies that no longer exist.[2] Most systems just wipe them when they disappear or merge. Instead, many analysts therefore take a sample of existing companies (ie, the successful ones) and look back at what happened to them exclusively. They do not include companies that existed at the beginning of their timeframe that do not now exist (ie, the losing companies).

Thankfully, there has been some academic research into the impact of survivorship bias. Most of this has been on the performance of mutual funds (ie, the US-grouped investment products bought by most people over there to invest for their retirement, in a similar way to our unit trusts and pension funds). It has become an issue because the industry has a habit of closing down funds that are not doing very well.

Now you see them, now you don't

Mutual fund companies may do this[3] to improve their statistics. If a fund is not doing well, it is closed, so the company only seems to have "successful" funds on all the databases you look at. Furthermore, others[4] have speculated that the industry also uses "creation bias" to help enhance their stats. To play this game, you start a number of funds and run them privately for a few years and just promote and keep the successful ones that then have a successful track record.

This behaviour is increasing according to research published by Martin Rohleder *et al* recently.[5] In 2006, over 6% of US mutual funds were closed. In the UK, a study published by the IMA in 2000 showed that half of the funds that had existed in the preceding two decades had since been closed down. [6]

Furthermore, TCF Investments suggest this has now become a bigger problem in the UK. In their 2011 report, "There's a Hole in My Bucket",[7] they showed that over the previous decade the UK fund industry had closed or merged about 10% of funds every year.

So, what effect do all these games have on the performance statistics? On the official ones, virtually none, as the analysis is done on surviving funds.

In practice, Martin Rohleder reviewed all previous studies and found they showed effects up to −2.7% loss of return per year for mutual fund investors. In their own comprehensive research of over 10,000 funds existing between 2003 and 2006, they found an average effect of −0.95%[8] per annum across a number of measures.

Why pretty models look so good

I am not aware of similar systematic studies quantifying the survivorship bias for investors buying individual stocks. However, some technical traders have tried to evaluate the impact it has on their models. For example, Frank Hassler showed how it could have a dramatic effect on the modelled returns from a simple trend-following strategy for buying/selling the 10 best stocks on the S&P 500.[9] Modelling just the current 500 constituents of the S&P index, his model projected returns of 24% pa. However, when he modelled correctly what would have happened in real life with all the companies that had actually been in the S&P 500 over that time (some 1,006 stocks), he found returns were significantly less at just 13% pa.

Given all this data (and particularly that from Martin Rohleder), I think a conservative estimate of the reduction that should be applied to equity returns due to survivorship bias is probably around −1%. It is quite possible the figure is different for individual share investments and funds, but there is just not enough reliable data to determine the exact numbers.

KEY LEARNING POINTS:

- Survivorship bias is an effect that exaggerates the returns on stock market investing by only analysing the results of successful companies or funds.
- As an example, I show how the returns of the top 20 companies in the FTSE in 2001 actually declined by –23% over the next decade while the index appeared to decline by just –3%.
- The effect has been quantified for funds, and is estimated to be around –1% pa.
- There is less evidence for its effects on private investors. It is therefore suggested that this –1%pa be used as a best estimate to deduct from all equity returns to account for this factor.

1. http://www.macgetit.com/4943/solving-problems-of-wwii-bombers/ (accessed 3/3/2012).

2. As example of this, I had to resort to looking in the microfiche copies of *The Times* newspaper in the British Library to compile the previous table of 2001 prices!

3. http://www.investopedia.com/articles/mutualfund/09/mutual-fund-liquidation.asp#axzz1l35DD6Hs (accessed 31/1/2012).

4. http://www.investopedia.com/articles/02/013002.asp#axzz1l35DD6Hs (accessed 31/1/2012).

5. Martin Rohleder, Hendrik Scholz and Marco Wilkens, 2011, "Survivorship Bias and Mutual Fund Performance: Relevance, Significance, and Methodical Differences", *Review of Finance,* 15(2), pp 441–74.

6. http://www.investmentuk.org/assets/files/press/2002/20021014-01.pdf (accessed 31/1/2012).

7. Supplied to the author by TCF Investments; published November 2011.

8. Note that this is equal-weighted results that take an average effect across all funds. They also publish stats using a value-weighted approach that show less of an effect. However, because failing funds tend to get smaller (due to their failure and people withdrawing money), it is the author's view that equal weighting is more valid.

9. http://engineering-returns.com/2010/11/16/sp500-survivorship/ (accessed 31/1/2012).

"I have been a member of Selftrade for many years, in the past they have brought in fees for not trading, which have cost me money as I have waited for my penny shares to show a profit. Now I will be paying again just for being a member [£35 a year]. My portfolio is small, some of my share values will not cover the amount being asked for."

Anonymous comment on a review website[1]

6

Costs – Share Trading

This chapter examines all the costs and charges that can affect the average investor trading in shares (trading commissions, stamp duty, taxation, etc).

I have always thought that costs and charges on trading seem minimal and don't matter much. Indeed, when I trade I focus on the price I am getting before I hit the "proceed" button – and only afterwards, when I see the confirmation, do I consider what the costs were. Furthermore, if you're like me, you probably don't even look at them on that page. They usually seem small enough to ignore.

However, as we'll see, such complacency could be costing you a lot of your potential profit because (on average) people trade more now than they used to a few decades ago. The situation is as bad for those who invest in funds, and who suffer fund fees, charges and commissions (see next chapter). There are multiple potential costs, so let's look at them systematically.

The pennies add up

To start with, there are trading commissions when you buy and sell a share. There has been a strong price war in the industry in the UK and many brokers now charge only £10–15 per online trade (and sometimes even less if you trade more).[2] The amount this represents of your trade clearly depends on the size of that trade. Many private investors buy and sell shares in batches of hundreds of pounds. So, for example, if shares were bought for £250 on a £12.50 commission, this would represent around 5%. Note, you need to double this to work out the total effect on your investment to include the commission to sell the shares later – ie, a total of 10% overall.

There is no published data on the average size of a trade by a UK private investor. My best guess from talking to investors is that it is probably around £1,000, meaning that the average commission paid is probably around 1.25% for each deal – ie, 2.5% to both buy and sell.

Spreads – I can't believe it's not the offer price

There is also a semi-hidden fee that we all pay, ie, the bid/offer spread. This is the difference between the prices offered for you to buy and to sell them at any point in time. It exists because it is the margin made by the market maker who matches all buy and sell orders. In highly liquid markets, he can be very sure he'll be able to match them almost immediately and so spreads tend to be quite small. For rarely traded stocks, he is taking a much greater risk as circumstances could change greatly before he is able to match the order. Hence a higher spread.

Looking at the FTSE this morning as I write,[3] the spread is around 0.1% for the top 100 but 0.5% across the whole of top 350 FTSE companies. Although many exchange-traded funds (ETFs) can have similar low spreads, less liquid ones such as those investing in emerging markets can also have higher ones – sometimes up to 3%. Furthermore, many other less-frequently traded shares and instruments also can have very high bid/offer spreads. For example, shares in building society/bank debt (called permanent interest-bearing shares, or PIBS) often have spreads of up to 15%.

However, the largest spreads tend to be found in the very small start-up companies listed on markets such as the Alternative Investment Market (AIM).[4] For example, the very first share[5] alphabetically listed on AIM this morning has a 40% bid/offer spread. To make the effect of this clear, if you buy £100 worth of shares and want to sell them immediately, you would make a loss of £40 (even before trading charges, stamp duty, etc). This means you are going to need this share to rise by 67% before you break even. That is quite a risk to take.

Given all of the above, I propose to use an average bid/offer spread of 0.7% for the private investor. This is because I am aware that many private investors frequently trade smaller more speculative companies and, for them, this effect will be much greater than you see from looking at the spread on the FTSE 100.

An expensive stamp collection

The other charge that affects investing in the UK is stamp duty. The current rate is 0.5% and is charged on pretty much all share purchases.[6] It is not payable by you directly for some pooled investments like unit trusts and ETFs, as the investment will already have paid it on your behalf. However, the charge is still potentially reducing the value of these investments to some extent.

It all depends how often you do it

To fully calculate the impact of the above factors on an individual's investments each year, you need to know how many times they trade on average. Barber *et al* quote that, between 2000 and 2003, the average turnover on the New York stock market was 97% – ie, traders on average hold each share they buy for about a year.[7] There is anecdotal evidence that new investors turn over their shares much more frequently than this. In my calculations for private investors, I'll assume a portfolio turnover rate of 100%, ie, they hold an average share in their portfolio for one year.

Tax free is not free

Although it is common now to find online trading accounts without fees in the UK, they are often still charged on accounts with the same brokers that attract tax benefits, such as ISAs and SIPPs (Self Invested Personal Pensions). For example, companies like Halifax and Fidelity currently charge a 0.1% pa annual fee on their ISAs, while others have flat annual fees, eg, Selftrade charges £35 – which could equate to 0.33% if you contribute your maximum allowance of £10,680. However, as we saw from the comment at the beginning of this chapter, this £35 can be a much greater amount if you only have a few hundred pounds in your portfolio.

For trading accounts for pensions, the charges can be higher still. There are two broad types of SIPP offered. For the simple discount stockbroker SIPP offered by big players such as Hargreaves Lansdown, you'll often be charged an annual fee of around 0.5%.[8] However, for more flexible SIPPs which allow you to invest additionally in other assets such as property, building society accounts, etc, you will often pay a flat fee. For example, Prudential currently charges a £425 annual fee and a set-up fee of £300. This annual fee equates to 0.4% for a £100,000 portfolio – ie, not that different to the rates charged on the simpler ones. Note there are a few SIPP providers[9] that offer them without annual charges, but this is still unusual, as there are administrative costs with running pensions that must be covered somehow.

In addition to the above, some online brokers charge inactivity fees on all types of account they run (even non ISA/SIPP accounts). For example, if you have less than £7,500 in a TD Waterhouse account and are buying and holding shares, you'll be charged £50 pa, ie an extra 0.7%+ per annum.

Finally, online brokers are also making money from you on any cash you hold in their accounts while waiting to invest it. Most pay near 0% interest on cash, so there is an opportunity cost to you of nearly 3% pa compared to what you could be earning in a top instant access savings account.[10]

Tax doesn't have to be taxing

Taxation on investments has become relatively simple compared to a few decades ago. There is now just one main simple tax on capital gains (CGT). For basic rate taxpayers, it is currently 18% and for higher-rate taxpayers it's 28%. However, what many fail to appreciate is the impact of your tax-free allowance (£10,600 currently).

For most small investors this means that any gains they make will never be subject to tax at all. Even in very good years when the market goes up say 30% (and they make about 20–25% after all the costs we are discussing in this book), you'd have to have a portfolio of in excess of £50,000 to trigger gains that require you to paid any CGT.

Furthermore, efficient tax planning has also resulted in other people having less CGT liability now. For example, someone with gains on an index tracker can effectively bank these before the end of the tax year and reinvest in a new (but slightly different) index tracker, thereby avoiding "bed and breakfasting" tax avoidance rules.[11]

Given these facts and that so many people use ISAs, I propose to largely ignore the CGT liability in my calculations.

Dividend income for UK basic rate taxpayers is effectively zero. However, higher-rate taxpayers have to pay 25% (or more at the higher additional rate). The average dividend on the FTSE is currently 3.5% and for normal higher-rate taxpayers, the tax charge will be 0.8% of their portfolio value if it is not sheltered in an ISA.

One thing to be aware of on tax. For those investing in funds, there is normally the option to invest in "income" units (which pay regular dividends) or "accumulation" units (where all dividend income is used to increase the value of the funds and your units). You might think the latter gets you around paying dividend tax. I did until a number of readers of the first edition pointed out my error. It does not. See a good article[12] on the subject on the Monevator blog.

Having said all that, because so many use tax free ISAs and pensions, I have assumed there is no impact of dividend tax in my calculations for the average investor.

KEY LEARNING POINTS:

- Trading commission charges to both buy and sell shares cost a typical small investor approximately 2.5%, assuming they trade in £1,000 deals. It clearly depends on trade size, and could be as high as 10% if they trade in batches of a few hundred pounds.
- Stamp duty adds a cost 0.5% to share purchases.
- Bid/offer spreads typically add costs of between 0.5% and 1% depending on whether you mainly trade FTSE 350 shares or a mixture that includes smaller ones, foreign ones or other share types such as PIBs. 0.7% is

estimated to be average for a private investor, though it could be a lot higher if you regularly trade AIM shares.

- Small investors can also face charges from their broker; for SIPPs, they are typically 0.5% pa.
- Due to the relatively high capital gains tax exemption threshold and the wide use of ISAs, the effects of this tax are negligible for many UK investors.
- However, those not using tax-free shells for their investments are paying on average 0.8% pa in dividend tax, if they are a higher-rate taxpayer.

1. Reviewcentre.com.

2. Costs are higher for certain trades and for those by phone, but these prices are typical of those charged to individual online traders in the UK in 2012.

3. February 1 2012, 10am GMT and excluding Chaucer Holdings (LSE.CHU), which had a spread of 61%.

4. The AIM allows for trading of shares of smaller companies on the London Stock Exchange.

5. 3D DIAGNOST IMAG (3DD.L).

6. Excluding paper transactions less than £1,000 using a stock-transfer form.

7. Brad M. Barber, Yi-Tsung Lee, Yu-Jane Li and Terrance Odean, 2005, "Who Loses from Trade? Evidence from Taiwan", University of California, Berkeley, working paper.

8. Assuming you want to invest in shares. If you just buy their specific funds, HL waive their charge.

9. For example, Sippdeal.

10. There is move by the FSA to make SIPP providers declare the interest they make from your money (see http://www.ft.com/cms/s/0/77ce94e4-6877-11e1-b803-00144feabdc0.html, accessed 12/03/2012).

11. http://www.fool.co.uk/Your-Money/guides/Capital-Gains-Tax-Minimising-CGT.aspx (accessed 5/3/2012).

12. http://monevator.com/income-tax-on-accumulation-unit/ (accessed 10/5/2012).

"Retail investors cannot easily measure the price of investing through the investment funds, in part because a significant element of this price is not disclosed at all."

FSA[1]

7

Costs – Funds

This chapter systematically examines all the costs and charges that specifically affect a person investing in funds. Not all the costs are disclosed or apparent to the private investor.

Funds are pooled investments where your money is grouped together with others and invested for you by an investment manager. The most frequently bought in the UK are unit trusts and the open-ended investment company (OEIC) funds offered by pension and life companies to their clients.[2] The main arguments given for investing in such products are they are simpler and less hassle for you, as someone else is responsible for deciding what to buy and sell. They also usually ensure you get a good diversification and so reduce your risk.

Unfortunately, balanced against this, the industry has gained a bit of a reputation for charging high fees and for continuing to deduct them even when their investments have performed badly. Furthermore, the UK fund industry charges more commission than do most other countries around the world. For example, the average declared charge on a UK fund was 1.63% in 2009 versus just 0.91% in the US.[3]

This may be beginning to have an impact on their sales. Here is a comment I recently saw on the *Which?* website by a potential investor: [4]

"Hidden charges have always put me off investing in funds. The sooner the charges become more transparent the sooner I might start to take an interest. The law needs to be altered such that all fees must be declared up front in black and white."

The commenter correctly identifies the issue. There are in fact multiplicities of charges on funds and many of them are not always apparent when you buy them.

Trading fees

Let's start with your purchasing costs. When you buy a fund you might pay a trading fee of £10–15, like you do with shares. But you might not. Some discount online brokers now no longer charge fees on trading funds to encourage you to use them (eg, Hargreaves Lansdown and Halifax). In addition, pension and life funds don't normally charge them either. Given this, I'm going to leave this factor out of the main cost calculation. However, note that many brokers still charge trading fees on funds, so my analysis is going to be slightly optimistic for an "average investor".

The 5% service charge added to your bill

When you buy a fund, they either have a "bid and offer" price (like shares), or have what is called an "initial charge". Either way, it is typically a potential charge of around 5% (but can be up to 7%). For someone paying a 5% initial charge, this is effectively a cost of around 1% pa spread over five years.

Historically, this charge was usually split between the fund company and the advisers – such as the independent financial adviser (IFA) or a salesperson – who persuaded the client to buy the fund, in the form of a commission. Although this practice still continues with people investing for a personal pension or a life fund with a company (eg, someone like Standard Life or Aviva), it has changed somewhat for users of discount online stockbrokers.

Due to competition, many of the discount online stockbrokers such as Hargreaves Lansdown and Barclays don't levy the full initial charge on some/all the funds that they want to promote. Therefore, if you are a prepared to: (1) use an online stockbroker, (2) select funds yourself, and (3) accept their restricted range, you can avoid the initial charge. However, some charge is often still paid by many.

In addition, a fund might have an "exit charge" as well, although thankfully this is now fairly rare. Also, many discount brokers (but not all) offer no transfer fees between funds.

However, the above charges still affect many fund investments with pension and life companies, and they can have a significant impact on their performance. Therefore, for our calculations in Chapter 9, I propose to assume a

2.5% commission is charged on average and that it is amortised over a period of five years – ie, 0.5%pa.

Levies and swingers

In addition, to the initial charge, there is another fee that is often charged to the purchasers of funds, called the "distribution levy". This is to cover the trading costs for going out and buying extra shares to add to the trust for you personally. It also ensures that existing unit holders are not paying fees because of you joining the fund. In practice, there are buyers and sellers on most days and therefore the manager may not need to go to buy shares (or at least not as many as the total value of your investment). For this reason, the levy is often much less than the theoretical cost of 0.5% stamp duty + trading costs.

Some companies don't operate a distribution levy, but instead operate what is called a "swing" system. In this, if the fund is generally expanding, they set a price for all buyers and sellers that reflects the value of the fund[5] plus a distribution levy. If the fund is contracting, you pay/receive just the value of fund less the levy. This can mean, if you buy during the euphoria of a market high and then sell during a downturn along with everyone else, you are doubly disadvantaged by this levy. Most trusts operate a distribution levy rather than a swing system, but to find out for sure, read the very small print or ask the fund directly before you buy.

In my calculations, I have assumed the distribution levy is zero, as for most it is usually quite a low figure. Again this means I am slightly underestimating the true cost of fund investing.

The industry tries to make it simple

However, the biggest cost with using funds is that you have to pay for their management. Successful fund managers can earn £1m a year alone.[6] To make it easier to compare funds, the EU forced the industry in 2004 to publish their total expense ratio (TER) – the total of their expected fund annual management charge (AMC), administration costs, profit, legal fees and audit costs. It has been increasing in recent years and, for an average UK fund, it is now 1.7%.[7]

The apparent upward rise of TER in recent years is also perplexing given that a number of their costs ought to be fixed in price (eg, audit fees). You'd therefore expect, as the fund size increases, that the TER ratio should become a smaller proportion. The exact opposite seems to be happening. As an example, take the Fidelity American Fund.[8] Its TER was 1.67 in 2008, and it is now 1.70. In the interim, the fund price has increased by about 40%. If its costs had remained the same, the TER should have declined to 1.0, not gone up.

Somewhat depressingly, the funds with the highest TER costs have also proven to be the least profitable. In a story in *Moneyweek* in October 2011,[9] they reported an analysis of UK funds which showed that those with the highest TER quartile underperformed those in the lowest TER quartile by 1.0% pa for "active" and "balanced managed" funds.[10] Therefore, paying fund managers more does not guarantee success in any way. In fact, quite the opposite.

Also included in TER is something called *trail commission*. This is the annual fee (usually 0.5% pa but sometimes more) that is currently paid out of a fund to the clients' IFA or broker for the full lifetime of their holding.[11] This can be a very key element of the profitability of organisations' marketing funds. As proof of this, some index-tracking funds have reduced or stopped paying commissions to intermediaries, as the evidence of these charges would be so apparent. On January 1st 2012, this caused brokers such as Hargreaves Lansdown to start to charge their clients a direct fee for holding such funds without trail commission.

This trend is also likely to continue. In December 2012, the Financial Services Authority (FSA) will bring in its Retail Distribution Review (RDR)[12] changes. This will stop all trail commission for new business from that date, and will clearly have major implications for many in the industry, particularly discount online brokers. It is currently estimated that a third of Hargreaves Lansdown's revenues (and an even greater proportion of their profits) come from these hidden commissions.[13] Expect all online brokers to start charging fees for holding many more (if not all) funds in the future. At the same time, funds themselves will then reduce their TER, so the net effect may not be that different for investors. Having said that, greater transparency of fees is almost certain to lead to reductions in them (see more on this in Chapter 15).

In the meantime, there is an ever-increasing trend (at least for discount brokers) to refund some or all of the trail commission to investors in what they call in marketing speak a "bonus". For example, as of 2012,[14] Alliance Trust Savings refund it all, while other such as Barclays don't refund any, and others refund or demand some other fee for refunding some (eg, Hargreaves Lansdown and Commfreefunds).

When is a "total" not a "total"?

Returning to funds themselves and their published fees, you'd think from reading their investor factsheets that the "TOTAL" expense ratio is something that includes all their charges. Well, no, it doesn't.[15]

TERs were invented under the auspices of the EU when they reformed the way trusts were marketed in 2004. It was meant to be part of the new "simplified prospectus" whose objectives[16] were to show investors "commissions" and all "other possible expenses and fees" in a "clear, concise and easily understandable way". Unfortunately, the implementation of this failed summarily – which will be discussed more later in this section and also in Chapter 16.

So what expenses ended up being excluded from the TER? These are listed in an EU directive CESR/10-67.[17] According to a recent report by TCF Investments to the HM Treasury,[18] it is missing 16 separate charges. The largest of these are transactions costs such as trading commissions, stamp duty, bid/offer spreads and something called "price impact".[19] We've already covered some of these earlier in the section for private investor. However, what are the estimates for these missing aspects for fund investors?

In a book published in 2001,[20] William Bernstein attempted to quantify the real costs of funds. He noted that even though the published TERs[21] at the time varied from 1.3% to 2.0%, the actual size of (all) expenses were between 2.2% and 9.0%! His average "small cap" fund had a TER of 1.6% but a real total cost of 4.1%pa.[22]

PTR – the hidden number they don't want you to know

To fully understand these costs, you need to know another bit of information that was also created by the EU in 2004, called the portfolio turnover rate (PTR) – ie, the number of times a year each share in the fund is effectively bought and sold.[23] Unfortunately, the self-regulating governing body of most UK retail fund managers, the IMA, has recently decided to remove this number from standard reports (see Chapter 16 for the full story on this). Therefore, getting a measure of it is now almost impossible.

Honestlybanking.co.uk recently described the state of affairs as follows: "*There is a much more prosaic reason why the investment industry wanted the portfolio turnover rate suppressed: profit. It's probably the oldest trick in the investment manager's book; a low annual management charge, but make up the difference by turning over the portfolio.*" [24]

The oldest trick continued – tying knots around PTR to make it disappear

If that was not bad enough, the FSA – in conjunction with the IMA – had previously adopted an unusual definition of PTR[25] whose origin came from the EU commissioner.[26] This definition (1) adds together all sales and purchases, then (2) deducts from this the sum of inflows and outflows from the fund, and then (3) divides this by the fund size.

This means that if a fund sells every stock and then buys them all again, it would have a PTR that equalled 200%, not 100% as you might expect. Further to that, you can get negative PTRs that are completely meaningless. Say a £1m fund does no transactions, but £1m gets added by some investors and at the same time £1m gets removed by some others. The fund still has £1m left in it and the manager has not bought or sold a single share. His PTR = –200%.

In addition, some funds appear to have PTRs that equal 1,000+%. How? If a fund at the end of each day puts its cash in the bank, this is also counted by this definition as a share transaction. But putting cash in the bank involves no fees, so it should be excluded, but it isn't.

The key objective of the original EU directive[27] was to "provide clear information…that can be easily understood by the average investor". The EU seems to have failed in implementing this vision.

Why did no-one in the finance industry point out to the EU that the US regulators (like those in many other countries around the world, including Australia) had been

85

successfully using a simpler calculation that actually works as the retail investor expects it? All they do is to take either the net amount sold *or* purchased divided by the fund size, and they ensure they exclude cash transactions. In this, when you sell all your portfolio and buy something else, PTR = 100%. You can't get negative numbers. You can't get 1,000%+.

It is extremely difficult to believe the finance industry were not aware of the issues and the possible consequences. As might have been expected, the net result was that the UK regulator decided in 2010 that it was not going to require members to show PTR anymore as it was misleading, and it was also removed from the latest EU regulations on funds.

Therefore, instead of the achieving the original objective of directive 2001/107/EC of complete and clear disclosure of costs, we are now arguably in a worse situation than before 2001 (see Chapter 16).

POSTSCRIPT FOR EDITION 1.1: Curiously in the latest report [37] published by the IMA's own statistics department, they're started using the correct US (SEC) definition of Portfolio Turnover Rate. This would appear to be an admission that PTR is not only a useful statistic but that their own (previous) definition of it is not the right one.

Calculating PTRs effects – making the best of a bad job

All of this means that interpreting any standard published statistics available for the UK market becomes highly dubious, and frankly meaningless. According to Morningstar, in the US the current PTR (using the "correct" definition) is 81% across all mutual funds. There is some research evidence[28] to suggest that this figure slightly exaggerates the effect, as it can be biased by a few funds with very large PTRs.

In the UK, Lipper estimate that the portfolio turnover rate (with the correct definition) of UK actively managed funds is around 60%, ie, slightly less than the US published figure. [29]

So, let's return to why this turnover figure is important and what it means for the hidden costs incurred by a fund. In a study published by the FSA in 2000, the hidden costs were estimated to be 1.8%, assuming a 100% (real) fund turnover.[30]

Since that time, commissions have come down and so have spreads to some extent. Indeed, SCM Private are now estimating that if a UK active fund had a PTR of 100%, it would have hidden costs of around 1%.

My calculations are very similar, and I estimate the missing factors (with 100% PTR) to also be about 1.0%, made up of:

- 0.5% stamp duty
- 0.2% commissions
- 0.2% bid/offer spread
- 0.1% price impact

Therefore, if we have 60% turnover here now, this means the best estimate for costs not included in the average fund TER is about 0.6%.

POSTSCRIPT FOR EDITION 1.1: In May 2012, the IMA have at last published[37] estimates for some of these missing values, ie stamp duty and commissions. They are almost identical to mine.

Others have pointed out that the extra costs are even higher for some funds.[31] For example, emerging market funds might have "missing" extra costs of more than double this level. Having said that, mention should be made of the lower expenses of passive tracker funds that aim to replicate the performance of an index such as the FTSE. They not only have very low TERs (average 0.6%) but also low turnover rates (and hidden costs) too.

What they do when your back's turned – they get their shorts on

Finally, the chasing of low fund fees does not always come without a "cost" to the investor. A recent study by SCM Private showed that many UK fund managers manage to reduce their fees by loaning out their shares to people who want to short the market.[32] In return, they get fees – estimated to be worth £850m a year in the UK.[33] Although this could potentially increase returns for fund investors (as the fund gets the loan fee), there are some major issues with it.

First, by definition, loaning out your stock to someone who is intent on forcing the price of that stock lower by selling it might reduce the value of your investments in that fund.

Second, the funds normally pocket a third or more of the fees themselves according to a recent investigation by the *Guardian*.[34] And, lastly, loaning stock is subject to "counterparty risk" – ie, the risk that the loaner becomes insolvent and when their assets are sold they are insufficient to buy back the shares they sold and return them to the fund. This is a real risk as the collapse and bailout of AIG showed in 2008.

I have ignored this issue in my calculations of returns, as I have been unable to precisely quantify its affects. My gut feeling, though, is that the net is negative due to the declining share prices caused by the shorting of their holdings.

Trimming the hedge, leaving nothing for the investor

Although this book is primarily for the private investor, a brief note should be made of the fees charged on hedge funds. Hedge funds are another pooled investment, but they are less regulated and so can use a variety of investment approaches, including shorting, which are not open to funds aimed at the normal private investor.

They are targeted at the high-net-worth individuals and also trustees of pension funds. The OECD estimate[35] about 20% of pension schemes use them in Europe, and they can hold up to 10% of their wealth in them – ie, if you're in a UK company pension scheme, it could be some of your money we're talking about here.

So, what are their charges like? According to the OECD, not only do they normally charge fixed fees of up to 1–2% (more if it is "fund of funds" type), they also charge a fee of 20% of any of the profits made. Therefore, if the fund does well, you get some return, but they get a lot. In contrast, if things go badly, they still take their cut and you take the risk and loss of capital. According to a recent book, the net result is that between 1998 and 2010, investors made $9bn from investing in all listed hedge funds.[36] In contrast, their managers (and their consultants) made a staggering $440bn (yes, I have checked those numbers, the managers took 98% of all the profits made).

Clearly these numbers are not going to be used in our calculations for retail investor accounts, but they do portray the level of abuse of fees that there is in the industry. To quote the author of the book mentioned above, Simon Lack, "Never in the field of human finance was so much charged by so many for so little".

KEY LEARNING POINTS:

- Most pension and life funds charge a 5% "initial charge", though many private investors using low-cost online brokers pay less than this (and sometimes nothing at all).
- For my calculations, I'm assuming an average 2.5% initial charge (spread over five years – ie, 0.5%pa).
- When you buy a fund you may also get charged a "distribution levy".
- Fund investors have to pay an average total expense

ratio (TER) of 1.7%. This figure has been growing over time.

- It currently includes "trail commission", which can be 0.5% pa of the TER (although this will be abolished in December 2012).
- However, the TER excludes many expenses of the fund. These can be best estimated from the portfolio turnover rate (PTR).
- Unfortunately, the UK fund industry has removed this figure from factsheets. The best estimate is that PTR is around 60% and so adds a further 0.6% to costs (and much more to some funds such as emerging market ones).
- The exceptions to high fund charges are passive index-tracking funds. Investors in these can have significantly lower expenses (sometimes even below 0.5%).
- The loaning of stocks in funds to shorters also probably contributes to a small negative return and increases fund risk.

1. Kevin James, "The Price of Retail Investing in the UK", FSA (http://www.fsa.gov.uk/pubs/occpapers/op06.pdf, accessed 1/2/2012).

2. Other pooled investments include OEICs, investment trusts and ETFs.

3. Lipper, "Fund Expenses: A Transatlantic Study", December 2009.

4.http://conversation.which.co.uk/money/investment-charges-fund-managers-more-transparency/ (accessed 27/03/2012).

5. The net asset value (NAV), ie, the total value of all the shares in the fund, less any liabilities, divided by the number of fund units.

6. http://www.telegraph.co.uk/finance/2941827/Business-profile-Bolton-is-bowing-out-for-high-notes.html (accessed 1/2/2012).

7.http://www.iii.co.uk/articles/21508/time-discover-true-cost-investing (accessed 1/2/2012).

8. This is a random fund I picked for which I could find the data. Why the American fund? The first listed in their very long annual report!

9. http://www.moneyweek.com/shop/issues/558 (accessed 1/2/2012).

10. The difference was not as great for the cautious sector, but still 0.6% pa.

11.http://www.telegraph.co.uk/finance/personalfinance/consumertips/8799554/Trail-commission-Whats-that.html (accessed 2/2/2012).

12. http://www.fsa.gov.uk/pages/About/What/rdr/index.shtml (accessed 17/2/21012).

13.http://www.telegraph.co.uk/finance/newsbysector/banksandfinance/8677936/Hargreaves-Lansdown-shares-fall-on-FSA-payment-rule-change.html (accessed 17/2/2012).

14. http://www.thisismoney.co.uk/money/investing/article-1718291/Pick-best-cheapest-investment-Isa-platform.html (accessed 2/2/2012).

15. There is now a move by Fidelity Investments to switch to a definition called total cost of ownership (TCO), which does attempt to include most of the missing elements – see Chapter 14 for a more detailed discussion of this (and their press release issued on 31/01/2012: http://www.realwire.com/releases/Fidelity-Calls-For-Industry-Standard-To-Make-Fund-Charges-More-Transparent accessed 2/2/2012). See also http://www.ft.com/cms/s/0/ 60bb43da-4b4c-11e1-a325-00144feabdc0.html (accessed 3/3/2012).

16.Directive 2001/107/EC: http://www.esma.europa.eu/system/files/ Dir_01_107.PDF (accessed 23/2/2012).

17. Section 5 of http://www.esma.europa.eu/system/files/10_674.pdf (accessed 2/2/2012).

18.http://www.ft.com/cms/s/0/60bb43da-4b4c-11e1-a325-00144feabdc0.html (accessed 1/2/2012).

19. Price impact is a phenomenon caused when large quantities of shares are bought. Market makers may not hold enough shares to complete the deal at the agreed price and so adjust it to complete the order.

20. William J. Bernstein, 2001, *The Intelligent Asset Allocator: How to Build Your Portfolio to Maximize Returns and Minimize Risks* (New York: McGraw-Hill Professional).

21. Large cap = large capitalisation, ie, stocks of companies with a market capitalisation of five billion dollars or more.

22. See http://www.frontierim.com/uploads/frontierinvestment management-whenisaternotater.pdf (accessed 1/2/2012).

23. This is my intuitive attempt to explain PTR in plain English. The actual definition is more complicated, as you'll see shortly.

24. http://www.honestlybanking.co.uk/what-every-charity-trustee-should-be-worrying-about-and-the-one-question-they-should-be-asking (accessed 23/2/2012).

25. https://fsahandbook.info/FSA/html/handbook/COLL/4/Annex2 (accessed 1/2/2012).

26.http://www.efama.org/index.php?option=com_docman&task=doc_dow nload&gid=6&Itemid=-99 (accessed 23/2/2012).

27. http://www.fsa.gov.uk/pubs/cp/cp04_18.pdf (accessed 23/2/2012).

28. http://www.ici.org/pdf/rc_v1n2.pdf (accessed 23/2/2012).

29. http://www.fundweb.co.uk/fund-strategy/issues/16th-may-2011/blind-spot/1031016.article (accessed 23/2/2012).

30. Kevin James, "The Price of Retail Investing in the UK", FSA (http://www.fsa.gov.uk/pubs/occpapers/op06.pdf, accessed 1/2/2012).

31. http://www.frontierim.com/uploads/frontierinvestmentmanagement-whenisaternotater.pdf (accessed 1/2/2012).

32. http://www.scmprivate.com/content/file/pressreleases/press-release-scm-private-stock-lending-release-01-september-2011.pdf (accessed 2/1/2012).

33. http://www.guardian.co.uk/business/2011/aug/31/stock-lending-short-selling (accessed 2/1/2012).

34. http://www.guardian.co.uk/business/2011/aug/31/stock-lending-short-selling (accessed 2/1/2012).

35. http://www.oecd.org/dataoecd/4/46/39368369.pdf (accessed 23/2/2012).

36. Simon Lack, 2012, *The Hedge Fund Mirage: The Illusion of Big Money and Why It's Too Good to Be True* (Hoboken, NJ: John Wiley & Son).

37. http://www.investmentuk.org/assets/files/research/20120504-imastatisticsseriespaper3.pdf (accessed 10/5/2012).

COSTS - FUNDS

"In our view it is better to hold cash and deal with the limited real erosion of capital caused by inflation, rather than hold overvalued assets and run the risk of the permanent impairment of capital."

James Montier, GMO asset allocation strategist[1]

8

The Correct Return on Cash

This chapter looks at the negativity of the industry towards "cash". It then examines more closely what the industry uses when it makes comparisons with cash. It shows that in many cases it is using an inappropriate benchmark as its definition, which is not even available to a private investor. Furthermore, when building society accounts are used in comparisons, the rates quoted usually underestimate those obtained by a private investor.

The comment on the previous page by James Montier is one of the few I have found by investment professionals that have anything positive to say about cash. Overwhelmingly, everything you read argues against holding it. This comment on The Motley Fool's "10 Steps to Financial Freedom"[2] is typical of those you'll read:

"Over periods of five years, the returns from shares have historically beaten cash around 80% of the time. Over 10 years, this rises to about 90%, and for 20-year periods, it's 98%. With

odds like that, investing for the long term remains one of best ways of building your wealth."

The main argument is one of poor returns. However, the industry also argues against holding it on the grounds of "missed opportunity risk", namely by not investing it you could have missed the chance to "strike the big one". It is also criticised currently for offering returns less than inflation.

The cash deal

The second criticism is true and likely to remain so for a few years, given the Bank of England's determination to keep interest rates low (to save a collapse in the housing market). However, we are living in some very unusual times and normally bank base rates exceed inflation by around 2%. Therefore, given *mean reversion* (the concept that most things in the economy normally revert to their historical averages), this situation and argument against cash will probably not hold for long.

Often the other issue with cash is one of taxation. Unless funds are held within a cash ISA (or in certain National Savings products), they will be subject to tax at source, which is currently 20% for basic rate taxpayers.[3] This makes obtaining a better-than-inflation return more difficult. Having said that, the author's own analysis of interest rates over the last 20 years shows that an investor using the best instant access accounts could still beat inflation by 2%, even after paying basic rate tax.

Holding cash in a stock trading account is different, which should be noted by all investors. In these, the broker often offers an interest rate of the base rate less 1% or 1.5% – at the time of writing in 2012, this equates to near zero interest.[4] It is clearly a disincentive to hold cash long term in such accounts, even when you suspect the market is declining. Also, if your account is an ISA or a SIPP, it is not possible to take it out temporarily and invest it in an ordinary instant access building society account.

When is "cash" not "cash"?

Given all the negativity about cash, let's look a bit more carefully at the data that backs up the claim about its low return. The Barclays Equity Gilt Study is one of the main sources of historical data on cash that is used by many financial companies. In the appendix are tables of building society returns going back to 1945, and the reader could easily be confused into believing that cash is actually building society returns.

In fact, as noted in Chapter 2, the report uses UK Treasury bills, wholesale instruments that are almost impossible for any retailer investor to buy (the minimum purchase is £½m).[5] They use the 91-day bill, which mirrors fairly closely the base rate. However, this is not what a typical investor might receive on their cash. Instead, they would normally use a building society account. Thankfully some financial providers (eg, The Share Centre)[6] do make a point of comparing the returns on shares with those of building society accounts and also try and compare them to higher-rate savings accounts. However, others (eg, the claims about cash returns on The Motley Fool referred to earlier), use the UK Treasury bill data.

I suspect the reason why the industry uses this source is that it is easily available and goes all the way back to 1900. Collecting the same information for ordinary savers accounts is much more complicated. Indeed, trying to define which account from which bank or building society to use is also fraught with issues – especially so now, given the industry's strategy of lowering rates on accounts after a short-term bonus rate has expired.

Data from accounts that no-one uses anymore

For building society data, Barclays originally used the average interest rate on an ordinary share account for data between 1945 and 1985. In 1986, it switched to using the rate on the Halifax Liquid Gold Account, and from 1998 (to present) the postal Nationwide InvestDirect account. It will come as no surprise to any UK investor, therefore, that the rates on these accounts over the last couple of decades have not been representative of those they see advertised and significantly underestimate the cash returns of real investors.

To make the size of this error clear, the Nationwide InvestDirect account dropped to 0.68% in 2009, and in January 2012 (as I write) currently pays just 0.2% interest.[7] In contrast, over that three-year period, instant access accounts from many providers have paid around 3%.

The discrepancy between the industry and real-world data started to be significant around 1990. The author has therefore reworked the building society data since that time.

The rates used were obtained by looking at the best buy tables in *The Times* in the first week of January every year from 1990 to 2011.[8] The best instant access rate was used.

The results show that, over the last decade, *the industry has been underestimating the building society returns by 1.3% pa compound. Moreover, the underestimate has been increasing over time and was 2.2% in 2011 (and is now 2.9% in January 2012).*[9]

"Cash" Returns Per Annum After Inflation (but before tax)

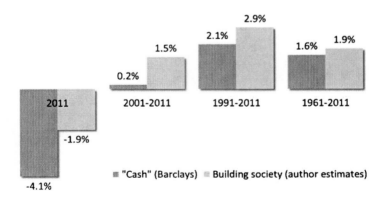

Based on data from: © Barclays Equity Gilt Study 2012 and author estimates

It's really taxing holding cash

The other aspect ignored in industry reports is that of tax. Compulsory basic rate tax is typically paid at source and this must be factored into comparisons where appropriate. The effects are quite marked and are of course even worse for higher-rate taxpayers.

The results show that, over the last 20 years – and even with paying the basic rate income tax – an investor in an instant access account would still have beaten inflation by 1.7% pa. For the longer term, the picture over 50 years is clouded by a period of hyperinflation in the UK in the 1970s (especially in 1975 when inflation peaked at 25%), distorting the figures.

The Effect of Tax on Building Society Returns (after inflation)

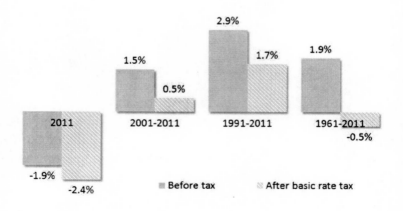

Based on data from: Author's estimates

There are exceptions where tax is not paid on building society interest (eg, cash ISAs, pension SIPP accounts, etc), so the industry should probably show building society rates on most charts with and without basic rate tax. Certainly, for many UK investors who are using ISAs for their stock market trading, the correct comparison should be the rates without tax, as they could have alternatively invested in a cash ISA.

KEY LEARNING POINTS:

- The industry is very negative towards you holding cash. They don't make money on it when you do.
- The only exception is when you hold it within a share trading account or SIPP, when they gain by paying you virtually zero interest rates (and get higher rates themselves).
- The industry is significantly underestimating the potential returns from cash in building societies when comparing returns with equities due to not using a typical account benchmark.
- The size of this underestimation is increasing and now stands at 2.9% pa.
- Industry comparisons usually ignore the effects of tax on cash and this can significantly reduce returns, as many have to pay it (unlike equity investing, where tax is more rarely paid).

1. http://blogs.reuters.com/reuters-money/2011/07/19/is-it-time-for-you-to-move-to-cash/ (accessed 30/1/2012).

2. http://www.fool.co.uk/10steps/step7.aspx (accessed 310/1/2012).

3. Higher taxpayers have an additional liability, making the total tax 40%.

4.http://www.ft.com/cms/s/0/38d8d73a-0a22-11e1-8d46-00144feabdc0.html (accessed 30/1/2012).

5. http://www.dmo.gov.uk/index.aspx?page=Gilts/Gilt_Faq#Treasury_bills (accessed 30/1/2012).

6. The Share Centre's "About Investing" guide, published in 2009 (available from http://www.share.com/a/investment-guides.html, accessed 30/1/2012).

7.http://www.nationwide.co.uk/savings/instant_access/investdirect/summary.htm (accessed 30/1/2012).

8. The logic for this method is that many people now use comparison tables and websites to select their accounts. I only used instant access accounts and returns assumed investors reviewed their savings every year in January and invested in the best account at that point.

9. The current best instant access accounts are offering around 3.1% (eg, West Bromwich, Nationwide, Santander).

"Fifteen years ago Michael Rundell started saving in a pension scheme with Scottish Life. In September 1994, the FTSE 100 was just above 3000. He paid into the plan every month, investing £70,000 in total. This month [October 2009], with the FTSE above 5000, he asked Scottish Life for the value of his fund. He was stunned by the reply. Despite the share index rising some 60% over the period, Scottish Life had turned the £70,000 into...just under £70,000."

Guardian Money, October 2009[1]

9

Equity Returns Revisited

In this chapter we'll summarise all the previous chapters and look again at the theoretical industry returns but this time factoring in the likely actual returns to a real investor. We'll then look at few scenarios of certain types of key investor and calculate their probable returns.

I have deliberately not tried to add up all the effects of the last few chapters as I wrote them. Instead, I have kept focused on researching each, one by one, and ensuring I have all my facts correct.

Literally just this morning, on my pad of paper by my computer, I have just totalled up the effects and I'm quite staggered by the size of it.

And the answer is…

… the picture does not look anything like that portrayed by the finance industry. Far from investing in the stock market resulting in gains of about 5% a year (above inflation), it seems that *the average real investor is missing nearly 6% per year from this and so is likely to be looking at a net loss of about 1% per year no matter how they invest.* Furthermore, most would have been better off just leaving their money in the bank, even at today's poor rates.

Factors reducing investors returns	Investors in shares directly	Investors in funds directly
Skill/alpha of the investor	−1.3%	−2.2%
Skill/alpha of a fund manager	n/a	+0.2%
Index error due to survivorship bias	−1.0%	−1.0%
Trading commissions	−2.5%	−0.1%[2]
Stamp duty	−0.5%	−0.3%
Bid/offer spreads	−0.7%	−0.1%
Initial charge/distribution levy	n/a	−0.5%[3]
Price impact	n/a	−0.1%
TER	n/a	−1.7%
TOTAL	−6.0%	−5.8%

Source: monkeywithapin.com

This table is a simplified summary of what we have found in the previous chapters, split by whether you are investing in the stock market directly or via managed funds like unit trusts. Somewhat bizarrely, the final result is almost the same, but how you get there is very different.

I cannot emphasise enough that this is a simplified summary. Different funds and different types of equity investments have different costs/potential benefits associated with them. For example, if you buy and hold a low cost index-tracking fund/ETF for 10+ years, your loss will not be 6%pa but less than 1%pa. Conversely, if you invest in emerging markets or "funds of funds" with higher real charges, your returns could be worse.

Also, the effects of trading commissions will be less if you trade larger amounts or you get special deals. Additionally, I have completely ignored the effects of taxation, which could add 0.8% alone to an individual investor's costs in dividend tax if you are a higher-rate taxpayer, let alone any capital gains tax.

Furthermore, all the above charges will be higher if you are investing in a pension. If you choose the SIPP route, you'll pay typical annual fees of around 0.5% pa. If you choose a personal pension, you'll usually pay higher initial charges of 5% typically, which over five years work out the same as the SIPP charge!

Cash is not such a bad investment after all

So let's now combine these numbers with those published by the industry and see what the equity returns would really look like for an average investor. It shows that, over the last 10 years, the average investor has not gained 1.2% above inflation but rather has lost 4.8%. In other words, even allowing for dividends, they may have been losing money in absolute terms – just as the example quoted in the *Guardian* at the beginning of this chapter showed.

True Returns on Equities vs "Cash"

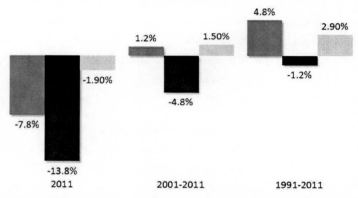

■ Theoretical equity return ■ Actual equity return ▨ Cash -Building society returns

Based on data from: Author's estimates and © "Barclays Equity Gilt Study 2012"

The analysis also shows that putting your money in an instant access building society account would have beaten investing in shares or funds for the average investor. Currently, this strategy might seem unwise due to the unusually low rates, but in the longer term it may not be.

Magician's trick #1: The inflating pension pot

I'm sure you're thinking that this cannot be true – someone would surely have spotted it before. The main reason is inflation. Factoring in inflation and doing compound interest calculations is beyond the skills of the average person in the UK. The effects of these costs are hidden and, provided we get back more in pounds than we put in, we think we have done well.

Not so well endowed after all

The trick has not worked so well when the finance industry has made some explicit promises about returns upfront. I'm thinking here of the low-cost endowment policies sold to millions of homeowners in the 1980s and 1990s. Most of these have never got anywhere near what was, at the time, projected to be their most pessimistic scenario (ie, the minimum death value payout).

As an example, I have one of these policies that I took out in February 1988 with the then best paying company, which matures after 25 years in 2013. The projected minimum maturity value at the time was £48,000.[4] To achieve this payout required only a return of 7% pa after charges. In 1988, this must have seemed pretty easy, especially as the industry regularly provided quotes to the public regarding projected increases of up to 13% pa at that time.

Let me illustrate the inflation trick exactly. I have paid in £17,250 and my policies' current value after 23 years is

111

£27,500. At first sight this may seem a good return – a growth of 4.2% pa. However, inflation averaged 3.5% during that time – ie, the policy beat inflation by a mere 0.7% pa – so it is effectively worth hardly more than I paid in. This is despite the investment period including a large chunk of the biggest stock market returns in recorded history and an average return of 5.7%pa above inflation.[5] In reality the fund lost 5% pa against the market and also did not get anywhere near paying out the absolute minimum projected at inception of £48,000.

This example clearly illustrates the effects of charges and commissions on returns (and also unrealistic sales projections from the industry). Note the 5% loss on my policy is not far off the sum of the charges estimates calculated in Chapter 6 and the index error due to survivorship bias in Chapter 5.[6]

As further examples of the inflation trick, let us look at three scenarios of a fictitious couple investing money for the last 20 years and what their returns might have been.

Story #1: Janet & John go investing[7]

Let's assume John has been assiduously investing £2,000 a year into a tax-free PEP from January 1st 1992 (and rolled it over to an ISA in 1999). Each year, he invested it in shares as an average investor does. He monitors the stock market a few times a day. He reads all the finance papers and magazines and is buying (and selling) stocks to gain as much as he can. He rolls over all those gains and dividends in the account and is always fully invested.

As a comparison, let's assume John's wife, Janet, is a bit more cautious and puts her £2,000[8] a year into a TESSA and then a cash ISA when they become available in 1999. Every year she reviews her policy on January 1st and transfers the balance to the best one being advertised at that point. So what would be their returns?[9]

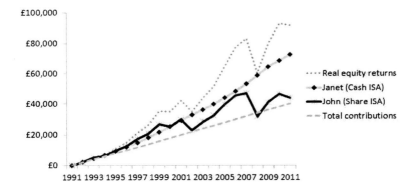

Source: monkeywithapin.com

John would have £44,019 from his total contributions of £40,000 since 1992. Therefore, if John was an average share investor, he'd have got back hardly any more than he put in. He'd have got a return of less than half a per cent a year with no allowance for inflation.

Compare that to what the industry says he should theoretically have gained from investing in the real stock market between 1992 and 2011: £91,950[10] – ie, a gain of 129% over this time period. Where did the missing £48,000 he was expecting go? *See the table earlier in this chapter for the answer.*

113

Now let's look at his wife. Janet spent virtually no time on her investments. She has better things to do in her life. She skims the rates in the weekend Money section in the first week of January (taking one minute). If the rate on her current ISA is not as good as the best rates at that time, she spends half an hour filling out an application form to switch providers. What does she get back? The answer is £72,493, a gain of 81% over the 20 years. Not as good as the industry says we could theoretically do on the stock market, but better than her husband – who spent all that time "playing" the stock market.

Moreover, if you look again at the graph, even at the peak of the stock market in 2007, John's ISA is still worth less than Janet's cash one.

Janet's gains each year are just over £1,600. They leave her more than enough to buy another pair of Jimmy Choo Lauren diamanté and suede sandals. In contrast, John's gains (just over £300 pa) are enough to buy a pair of hiking boots and some wet weather gear to walk across the moors alone and try to understand why his investing went wrong again that year.

Story #2: Janet and John are going to retire

Janet and John are aged 45 in 1992 so, instead of putting their money into an ISA, they decide to save for their retirement in 20 years' time.

John talks with an insurance company. They tell him he should have a personal pension as the returns will be at least 9% pa. He can choose to invest in funds that invest in

114

the stock market,[11] which have increased on average 14% per year over the previous 10 years, he is told.

So John decides to contribute his £2,000 pa to such a scheme and chooses a managed fund each year from those offered by his insurance company in which to invest his new cash. John keeps an eye on his investments once or twice a year when he reads his statements or he notices news headlines about the stock market crashing. He panics sometimes when the market goes down and switches funds to less risky ones and then back to equities when they recover. Thankfully, his pension fund lets him off any switching fees. When he invests new money, he often picks funds that seem to be doing very well. In other words, John acts like a normal pension fund investor.

As a comparison, Janet sets up a SIPP account[12] to invest her £2,000 a year. She leaves the money in it as cash, earning just the base rate of −1%.[13] She doesn't even attempt to invest it anywhere and is lucky enough to have picked a provider that does not charge her inactivity fees or an annual fee.

So, when they come to retire at the age of 65 in 2012, how big are their pension pots?

John's pension pot at the end of the 20 years is worth £45,507. It is worth slightly more than if he'd invested the shares in his ISA in individual shares. Despite being deducted a 5% initial charge on everything he puts in and for annual management fees, his trading costs are much lower due to using a group fund, so he gains slightly more overall.

How does John feel about this, do you think? He was told by the insurance company in 1992 that he would get back a return of about £161,000 – ie, about a 300% gain. He has in fact gained just 13%.

Janet, on the other hand, left her cash uninvested in a SIPP. She was heavily penalised by the stockbroker for not investing it, with a derisory interest rate of base rate less 1%. However, her investment of £40,000 did at least make some money over the 20 years. In the initial years, base rates were significantly higher than they are now and she obtained a positive rate of interest. Her pension pot is worth £55,814.

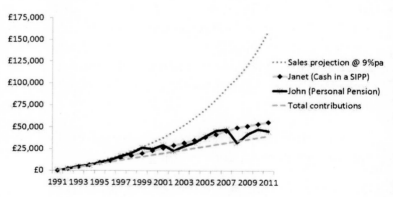

Source: monkeywithapin.com

Unfortunately, Janet also thinks that her pension was probably not worth bothering with. She could have decided instead to forego the tax relief of putting the money into her pension. Then, as in scenario #1, she would have been able to put the money into an ISA. In that scenario, even after paying basic rate tax and NIC first, and investing less money each year, she'd have got almost the same money back as she did with cash in the SIPP. However, unlike the pension pot, she'd not now be tied into buying an annuity at an extremely poor rate and be free to spend it how she wished (ie, on a complete new wardrobe of Jimmy Choo shoes).

Interestingly, there has also recently been a debate[14] in the industry over whether it is worth investing in a pension at all and that, for some people, an ISA might be better – particularly if they are younger and a basic rate taxpayer.

Finally, the above examples are not saying you can't be lucky because of your timing and equity selections and beat these returns. Indeed, half of you will have done better than this, and a few much better. I sincerely hope that you are among that group and not the other half who did worse than these examples.

Magician trick #2: The ever so small that it hopefully disappears act

So we've looked at the "inflation" trick as an explanation of why people have never noticed the impact of this 6% before. There is another reason that this underperformance of equities has not been more widely discussed: the "so small to be insignificant trick". The size of the charges we are talking about seem quite small to the average person.

They reason "how can a few per cent here or there in commissions really make much difference to me when equities perform so well over the long run?"

Hotel maids are at it

I read a novel once where there was a scam in a hotel; one of the maids was stealing tiny amounts of money from each person's room. It worked for a very long time and the maid eventually became very rich from it. No-one complained, as they could not be sure they had lost such a small amount and most never even noticed.

This seems to offer a good parallel with how the UK finance industry has worked. By taking a very small percentage annual charge or transaction fee from everyone, they become rich beyond their wildest dreams, while no-one has really noticed or worked out how.

So how do the small percentages add up to so influence your returns? It is partly because the amount taken, although small, is actually a large proportion of the long-term return of equities. However, more importantly, it is the compound effects of the lack of that money that matters. Remember how we showed that returns from investing had little to do with the capital growth of the FTSE (after inflation) but almost all to do with the ever-growing 4.5% pa average dividends. Let's look at another example to make this clear.

Story #3: Janet and John get an inheritance

John has just received an inheritance of £10,000 from his late mother. He is not quite sure what to do with it, as he doesn't need the cash right now, so he and Janet walk into a LloydsTSB branch on the high street. Let's imagine the bank tells him to go for a stock ISA, as it is ideal for long-term savings. However, he does have one decision to make. He has to pick a fund. John has no idea which one to choose, so goes for the one they used as an example for the charges in the book, as it looks like it will make him lots of money. He selects the Scottish Widows UK Growth Fund.

So what would the book say? Scottish Widows use the FSA standard table of projected returns, which say 7% growth for a fund ISA.[15] It also clearly states there are TER expenses of 1.61% for that fund, which I'm sure John did not think were a big deal.

The current key features pack[16] then projects this forward having taken into account the official TER expenses. This clearly says that his £10,000 will grow to be about £15,900 after 10 years. This will show Janet that he can be a clever investor.

The table also shows the effect of their official charges (the TER and the 5% initial charge fee) – ie, he will lose £3,760, ie, nearly 40% of the potential gains. That is a lot to have lost from his final returns from what seems like an innocent 1.61% TER and the initial charge, but John does not really bother as he is focused on the £5,900 he is probably going to make.

However, as we've noted earlier, John's fund is most likely not going to perform as well as the long-run UK equity return rate, because it is missing a deduction for survivorship bias of –1% pa. In addition, the official fees miss those related to portfolio turnover. The current brochure states this to be about 50%. This therefore makes an extra 0.5% pa that needs to be deducted to cover stamp duty, commissions, bid/offer spreads and market impact.

So what is John likely to get back in 10 years' time? The true picture is worse than his expectations. His £10,000 will probably grow to just £13,625, ie, he will lose £6,035 (about 60%) of the potential gains he could theoretically have received.

To make matters worse, let's say inflation averages 5% over the next 10 years. He will then have lost purchasing power too, as £10,000 now should be worth £16,290 then with inflation added.

**£10,000 Investment in Scottish Widows
UK Growth Fund ISA**

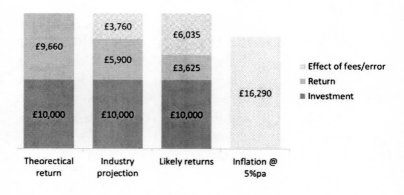

Source: monkeywithapin.com

Barclays mortgage dept agrees

Now for a postscript. Barclays mortgage department have published an even more pessimistic analysis than the one I have presented above. According to the *Sunday Times* today (February 12th, 2012), they are so certain that the returns on investors' stock ISAs will be zero in absolute terms over the next 25 years, that all new Barclays "interest only" mortgages have to assume that investors using ISAs to pay them off have to work on only the capital remaining in them after 25 years will be that paid in.

Therefore, in the above example, Barclays would be now assuming you just get back the blue £10,000 you put in. No green area returns at all.

Q.E.D.[17]

In the following section we look at the implications of these findings for individual investors, the finance industry and regulators. Finally, please note that I'm not advocating you stop investing, just that you do it more cost efficiently and with more knowledge about the facts.

KEY LEARNING POINTS:

- The real returns for the average investor are significantly less than the theoretical published equity index by about –6%.
- Aggregating the data from the previous chapters, this means that the long-term return for equities is not +5% pa but –1% pa, after accounting for inflation.
- Indeed, inflation is probably the reason that the

industry has managed to hide these facts for so long, as it is less apparent on absolute returns.

- The examples provided show that, for the average person investing over the last 20 years, they will probably have been lucky to have gained much at all in absolute terms (and certainly not match inflation).
- Note these are average figures for all UK investors. Some will have been luckier or more skilled and made money. In addition, some funds and strategies have suffered from lower costs and so also made more money (see Chapter 13 for more on this).
- Finally, the industry itself is beginning to realise the truth of these facts. Barclays mortgage department is now assuming that future stock ISA investors will only get back the cash they paid in after 25 years of investing effort (and charges).

1. Guardian News & Media Ltd, 2009
http://www.guardian.co.uk/money/2009/oct/03/investment-funds-fit-for-purpose (accessed 1/2/2012).

2. I have assumed you are using one of the few discount online brokers that does not charge commission to trade funds. If you are not, subtract a further 2.5%!

3. I have assumed that the distribution levy is negligible. This will not be the case for everyone.

4. Premium is £750 pa, including an estimated £50 pa for the term insurance element. The term insurance element has been excluded from all returns calculations.

5. *Source:* Barclays Equity Gilt Study 2011.

6. It excludes "alpha", as there is no timing errors or fund selection errors in this type of investment.

7. After the famous Janet and John children's books (see http://en.wikipedia.org/wiki/Janet_and_John, accessed 23/2/2012).

8. To be strictly accurate, she could not have put in £2,000 in 1996 but would have to have contributed just £1,000. She would have been capped by a £9,000 limit over five years for that year but, for the sake of the simple comparison, I've ignored that.

9. Assuming the instant access building society account rates. Historically, this is probably an understatement of the real returns.

10. *Source:* Barclays Equity Gilt Study 2011.

11. The stock market had gone up 14% pa for 10 years (including the big downturn of Black Monday), so projecting 9% pa was conservative then.

12. The first online SIPP was introduced in 2000 by Sippdeal. So this comparison is slightly artificial as SIPPs did not exist in 1992. However, as an example of the possible effects on future returns, it is useful.

13. Interest rate assumed never to be negative.

14. http://www.investorschronicle.co.uk/2012/03/01/comment/smart-money/isas-versus-sipps-which-wins-k033wxmDJl3s95PyWUInvO/article.html (accessed 5/3/2012).

15. I assume the FSA's logic behind the 7% is that the long-run equity return rate is 5% + inflation, which is targeted at 2%.

16.http://reference.scottishwidows.co.uk/literature/doc/SW56494b (accessed 20/2/2012).

17. QED = *quod erat demonstrandum*, from the Latin – which translates as "as was to be expected". The phrase is traditionally placed at the end of a mathematical proof or philosophical argument to signal the completion of the proof.

Part II: The Implications

This section will now look at the consequences of the evidence presented in the first section. It looks at a set of implications for private investors covering whether to hold cash, how to cut investing costs, how to change your trading behaviour, the best strategies, and the benefits of different types of investments and that of other assets classes.

It then looks at implications for the finance industry and regulators. Finally, I'll conclude with my own take on it all.

"The reason I started investing in shares was that building society rates have been so low, which left me thinking what the point in investing say £1,000 and getting back 5% if you were lucky. Obviously, one wouldn't even get that now."

Colin, recent share trader

10

Implications for Investors #1 – Cash

In this chapter we look at the potential benefits and issues with holding more cash than traditionally would be recommended in your portfolio.

One of the things that surprised me most while researching this book was that investing in shares had not beaten putting the money in the building society, particularly over the last 10–20 years. This finding is certainly at odds with statements on many investing websites.

I suspect the origin lies in fact that most people in the industry now advising the public were around in the 1980s and 1990s, when stocks really did consistently deliver 15–20% returns a year. To them, this proposition must still seem so obviously true that they will regard anyone like myself challenging it as a knave and a fool.

Anchors away

However, I would suggest that they are suffering from a cognitive bias called *anchoring*.[1] The evidence of history suggests that they happen to have been working in an extraordinary couple of decades, the like of which we may not see again for a long time. This has created a frame of reference – based on their career during a boom time – that such a situation will continue forever. As we saw in Chapter 2, the UK stock market index (excluding dividends and allowing for inflation) went nowhere for 90 whole years before they got a job in the city in 1980s.

Keep the divis coming in

The return that historically comes from investing comes almost solely from the dividends and not from capital growth. The average annual dividend yield from the FTSE All Share Index is 4.5%[2] over the last 112 years. It currently stands at 3.25% (as of February 2012).[3] Moreover, we have seen in Chapter 9 that the penalty for private investors for holding shares is up to 6% pa, making returns from dividends alone rarely likely to be a break-even strategy versus cash.

Cash is good

Given this, there may be an argument to consider holding some or even all of your wealth in cash. Furthermore, normally interest rates on cash are higher than dividend rates. The average is 5.3% since 1900.[4] Even allowing for paying tax sometimes, the returns will be higher than that of equities in the long run (as we saw in Chapter 5). This is due to the penalty of 6% for that investment class.

There are also a number of benefits of holding cash over shares, at least some of the time, as some journalists have recently pointed out (eg, Bengt Saelensminde).[5] These can be summarised as follows:

- *Cheapness:* There are generally no fees/transaction costs with cash (unlike shares – see previous chapter).
- *Simplicity:* A savings account is easy to understand. Everyone knows how the system works and can be transacted in person on the high street.
- *Low risk:* Unlike shares and other investments, in theory the value of your holding cannot go down. Despite the bad publicity about bank failures, holding cash in a bank or building society is still pretty safe – with the government guaranteeing funds of up to £85,000 per banking group through the Financial Services Compensation Scheme.
- *Optionality:* You normally have the ability to take out your investment easily and invest it elsewhere should a better opportunity arise. This might be when others offer higher rates of interest but also includes investing in the stock market when prices are genuinely very low (see Chapter 13).

Or is it?

So what are the main issues with holding cash? They are probably threefold:

- *Tax.* The main downside of holding cash is that it can be subject to a higher rate of tax than equities. Most savings accounts are taxed at source at 20% and higher-rate taxpayers may have to pay 40% (or more) currently.[6] This compares with equity dividend income tax rates of effectively zero for basic rate taxpayers and 25% for high-rate ones.

The simplest way to avoid paying tax on cash is to hold it within a tax-free environment, eg, National Savings Certificates, a cash ISA or a SIPP pension. Clearly, there are limitations on how much money can be invested in such schemes, but for the average UK saver, they afford ample opportunities to keep cash with tax-free returns.

There is a further problem about holding cash within a SIPP pension that we've already mentioned. In most low-cost SIPP accounts, the rate of interest paid on cash is usually extremely low – currently approximately zero and, during more normal times, is usually 1–1.5% less than the base rate. To get around this problem, you need to choose a more expensive and more flexible SIPP product that typically makes an annual charge of a few hundred pounds.

In these, you are permitted to invest tax-free directly into building society accounts or accounts such as National Savings. Your SIPP savings accounts have to be run as trustee accounts and so must be postally administered. Unfortunately, this severely restricts your choice of account[7] and will exclude many Internet-only deals you see advertised. That said, you will be able to nearly match the best buy rates.

- *Risk*. Until 2008, few savers stopped to consider the potential risks of putting their cash in a bank. However, following the demise of Northern Rock and various Icelandic banks, we are now all too aware of this issue. That said, provided you ensure that you keep accounts below a limit (currently £85,000) in each banking group, the UK Financial Services Compensation Scheme will guarantee it.[8]

- *Low interest rates*. This is probably the key issue in my view. It is certainly the reason that has caused many to start investing the stock market recently. Not only have the governments of the UK and US promised to keep interest rates low for the next couple of years, history also suggests that this will happen and last much longer than currently expected by many. After the last great credit crisis of the 1930s depression-era, UK interest rates never got above 2% for 20 years.[9] It could be argued that the Second World War helped suppress them for longer, but it is not impossible the UK could see low interest rates for at least a decade.

Currently, the best instant access savings rates are around 3% and 4.8%[10] for five-year bonds. These are all less than the current RPI inflation rate of 4.8%.[11] Despite the fact that inflation may fall in 2012, its long-term trend is up (see CPI inflation graph below), and there are many reasons to suspect it may be unofficial government policy to let it do so, to erode the value of its debts.[12]

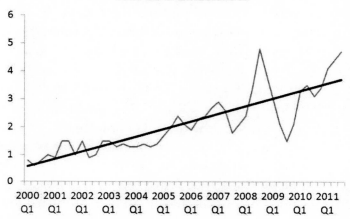

Based on data from: Office for National Statistics

Indeed, a recent paper by Carmen Reinhart and Belen Sbranci[13] showed how the UK government and those around the world have been using this trick of low interest rate and high inflation – called *financial repression* – to deal with debt crises since Napoleonic times. It relies on the illusion where people focus on nominal interest rates and don't work out the inflation-adjusted ones.

Given this, interest rates on savings accounts are probably not going to match inflation for a long time yet.

I'm confused. Is it good or not? Ask a monkey

So where does this leave you as an investor – a fixed loss with cash or variable, but potentially a bigger or smaller loss with equities? To me, this seems like the classic loss-aversion[14] experimental scenario and also very similar to one which some people recently tested on monkeys (rather appropriately given the title of this book).

Laurie Santos and colleagues at the Comparative Cognition Laboratory at Yale University have been running a number of experiments with capuchin monkeys over the last decade. In their most recent work,[15] they gave their monkeys one of two choices when they got their food. They could get a sure loss, ie, be presented with three pieces of apple but always handed over two. Alternatively, they could have a risky loss, ie, be shown three pieces, but sometimes delivered all three and other times given just one. The results should not be surprising to you as a share trader. The monkeys were so willing to avoid loss that they preferred the risky dealer 71% of the time.

That makes me think that, despite the logic and maths of the arguments in this book that cash returns will probably outperform equities for the average private investor in the next five years, most people will still want to invest in shares because they cannot bear to accept the guaranteed loss, after inflation, of their putting their money in a savings account.

Finally, just a quick word about asset allocation[16] in relation to cash. Traditional financial advisors would often suggest keeping a small amount of your portfolio in cash – maybe 5–10%. However, all asset classes now seem to be highly correlated in a "risk-on"/"risk-off" way (ie, when shares go up, so can commodities and bonds). Therefore, some[17] have been arguing that you should hold a higher proportion in cash, eg, 25%. Furthermore, in these turbulent times for equities, it also has "optionality", ie, allows you to easily exploit opportunities to invest when other assets become cheaper (see Chapter 13 for a further discussion of this strategy). All of this I think could argue for greater cash allocations in portfolios (see Chapter 15 for a more detailed discussion on asset allocation).

KEY LEARNING POINTS:

- Historically, savings interest rates have been higher than share dividend yields. Bank interest rates have averaged 5.3% since 1990 versus just 4.5% dividend rates.
- Furthermore, there are number of potential benefits of holding some cash: cheapness, simplicity, low risk and optionality.
- The main issues with holding cash are: tax (although not in ISAs or SIPPs), capital risk (if holdings >£85,000) and low interest rates.
- If history repeats itself, interest rates will remain low for potentially a decade or more. At the same time, inflation may well be high, so staying in cash will lose purchasing power.
- However, the loss will be known and fixed, unlike real investors equity returns which, after deducting 6% pa, may well be lower still.
- There could be arguments for holding more cash in a portfolio now due to the correlation of asset classes

and the need to maintain optionality for future investing opportunities.

1. Anchoring is the tendency to rely too heavily (or "anchor") on a past reference or on one piece of information when making decisions.

2. *Source:* Barclays Equity Gilt Study – arithmetic average. Note they only adjusted their benchmark to cover the FTSE All Share Index in 1962, while historically it covered just the FT 30 index. However, there appears not to be great difference in yield rates between these two periods with different definitions.

3. *Source: Financial Times*, 8/2/2012. Note that some would argue this low dividend yield is a reflection of the continued overvaluation of the stock market following the massive bull market of the 1980s and 1990s.

4. *Source:* Barclays Equity Gilt Study 2011 – arithmetic average of annual Treasury bill rate. Note this is defining cash from Treasury gilts, which we know underrepresent building society rates (see Chapter 8).

5.http://www.moneyweek.com/investment-advice/how-to-invest/strategies/five-good-reasons-to-hold-cash-56816 (accessed 30/1/2102).

6. With those earning over £150,000 paying 45/50%.

7. See http://www.investmentsense.co.uk/tag/sipp-deposit-accounts/ for a list of potential options and current rates (accessed 8/2/2012).

8. http://www.fscs.org.uk/ (accessed 8/2/2012).

9. During that time the Bank of England base rate remained at just 2% except for a two-month period in 1939 (see http://www.bankofengland.co.uk/statistics/rates/baserate.pdf, accessed 8/2/2012).

10. http://www.comparethemarket.com/compare-savings-accounts/ (accessed 8/2/2012).

11. http://www.bbc.co.uk/news/business-16591740 (accessed 8/2/2012).

12. I am well aware of the many deflationist arguments related to fiscal contractions and recessions. However, the UK is printing vast amounts of money that will eventually lead to more inflation either directly or indirectly via reductions in the value of the pound.

13. Carmen M. Reinhart and M. Belen Sbrancia, 2011, "The Liquidation of Government Debt", working paper, March (see http://www.imf.org/external/np/seminars/eng/2011/res2/pdf/crbs.pdf).

14. Loss aversion is the tendency to strongly prefer avoiding losses to acquiring gains. Some studies suggest that losses are twice as powerful, psychologically, as gains.

15. V. Lakshminarayanan, M. K. Chen and L. R. Santos, 2011, "The Evolution of Decision-making Under Risk: Framing Effects in Monkey Risk Preferences", *Journal of Experimental Social Psychology*.

16. Asset allocation is an investment strategy that attempts to balance risk versus reward by adjusting the percentage of each asset type (eg, equities, bonds, cash, commodities) in an investment portfolio according to the investor's risk tolerance, goals and investment timeframe.

17.http://www.moneyweek.com/investment-advice/how-to-invest/strategies/the-right-side-investment-asset-allocation-14900 (accessed 8/2/2012).

"Doing nothing is invariably more profitable; a lesson that I am continually reminded of. But suffering from the human requirement to be doing something, I seem to struggle with this aspect of investing. This is my single most important lesson IMO and my resolve has strengthened in this regard – perhaps I can aspire to reaching a threshold of inactivity that is finally productive in 2012 ;-)

John, private investor

11

Implications for Investors #2 – Cut Your Costs

The results of Chapters 6 and 7 showed that the biggest area of losses was related to charges. In this chapter we therefore focus on exactly what the private investor can do directly to reduce their costs. We also look at whether spread betting might be a solution.

As I mentioned in Chapter 6, I have personally always largely ignored the charges when I trade. They appear on my confirmation, but these just get filed (or ignored on the basis that they are always online somewhere if I need them). I'm sure I'm not alone in thinking that I will make so much on my trades that they are pretty immaterial. Unfortunately, I then go on to stop–loss a proportion of those trades out, so suddenly they no longer become so insignificant.

You should have listened to the fools after all

Moreover, I was genuinely quite shocked to do the analysis to see how big an effect they can have on your portfolio. Like many, I have read often enough that you should not to trade so much. Indeed, the quote at beginning of this section is a good example and one I saw a few weeks ago online, written by someone reviewing their portfolio at the beginning of 2012.

So what exactly can we do to help reduce the costs outlined in previous section? You cannot easily avoid stamp duty costs or the bid/offer spread, so the bulk of your efforts should be to reducing trading costs and fixed fees from your broker. Below are my 10 top tips for people trading shares or investing directly in funds.

TEN TOP TIPS TO SAVE ON YOUR COSTS

1. Ensure you are using an Internet stockbroker and *trade online* with them. If you buy shares over the phone, you usually pay £20–40 per transaction and so your annual trading costs could easily escalate to near 10% pa[1] on this element alone.

2. Make sure you are *paying no more than £10–12 per trade.* Some charge by a percentage – work out what this will be for your likely size of trade and compare it to these values. There are special deals for more frequent traders[2] and sometimes you can pay a fee and get a certain number of free trades. Only take those up if you are sure you need such deals and that they'll be cost effective for you. Remember, you should be cutting

---

down on trading!

3. Read the *small print on their charges* and avoid brokers who charge any of the following: annual fees, inactivity fees, trading commission on funds, etc.

4. *Beware SIPP/ISA account charges.* If you want a SIPP (to trade shares/funds in, as opposed to putting cash in a building society), you should be able to get one for free – ie, no set-up charge and no annual management fees. Trying to find a free ISA trading account is more difficult, but possible.

5. If you're *trading funds,* ensure you don't pay any initial charges and that you get as high a rebate of the annual trail commission as you can. Ideally, all 0.5% of it. Avoid providers who charge you fees to invest in lower-cost funds.

6. Don't think avoiding buy/sell trading commission by *using a fund* is necessarily better than share dealing. You may still pay substantial amounts in management fees and other hidden costs over the long run.

7. Before definitely deciding to buy a share, consider its *bid/offer spread.* If it is >1%, think carefully about it, and if >5% really challenge yourself over how much money you are going to make after costs.

8. If you want to get exposure to *international markets* (especially the US), consider doing it *via a fund* rather than investing directly. You will largely avoid foreign exchange commission and also not get withholding tax on dividends/double taxation problems. In addition, hidden fees on US funds tend to be lower.

9. Try and trade in *as large a size of transaction* as you can

afford. Remember, you need to be trading in volumes of over £5,000 to get your buy/sell commission down to below 0.5%. Really try and avoid buying/selling amounts less than £500 (ie, 5% commission).

10. Lastly, the single most important thing you can do to cut your costs is to *trade less*. Indeed, review your last year's transactions now. If your portfolio turnover[3] is >100%, consider the impact of this. For example, if it is 200%, your total trading costs have potentially risen from 4% to 8% of your portfolio value that year (assuming a £1,000 average trade size).

Women are just better than men. Full stop.

The effects of "over-trading"[4] on returns have been well documented in a number of studies. Interestingly, it is one of the reasons that women often make more successful traders than men. Women think through their actions more than men (ie, do more research and ask more questions) and as a result do less trades. Think back to that typical story from Iqbal who rushed out and bought a portfolio of shares as soon as he set up his trading account.

Barber and Terrance Odean published a paper in 2001 entitled "Boys Will Be Boys".[5] Using account data for over 35,000 households from a large discount brokerage between 1991 and 1997, they analysed the investment patterns of both men and women. They found that men traded 45% more than women. Moreover, men's trading reduced their returns by 1% per year compared with women.

Interestingly, they note that if the men had to ask their wife's permission to trade first, their performance increased. I make no comment...!

The great sage of Omaha, Warren Buffett, may not be of the fairer sex, but he certainly acts like one when it comes to trading.[6] He keeps Berkshire Hathaway's portfolio turnover as low as he can. You should too.

Spread betting saves costs but at what price?

Although this book is primarily about share and fund investing, I thought I'd touch briefly on spread betting as, at first sight, it appears to cut out many of the costs associated with share trading.

Spread betting involves betting on whether something (an index, a share, a commodity or whatever) is going to go up or down. The system is a simple one of betting a certain amount per point change. If the item goes in the direction you expect, you get the change in points times the amount you bet. If it goes the other way and against you (and you stop your bet), you owe the change times the amount.

This has the obvious benefit of allowing you to profit from both rising and falling markets, and is very much an extension of the Contracts for Difference (CFDs) that have existed for a long time. Also, being leveraged, you can potentially make very big gains from small stakes.

In the context of this book, there appear to be a number of benefits to spread betting compared to buying shares or index funds, mainly in relation to costs. You not only don't pay stamp duty or trading commissions, but spreads are usually very small. Further, if you do make profits, they are tax-free (as it is gambling). So almost 3.7% of the missing 6% from share dealing is eliminated. Survivorship bias is also unlikely to affect spread betting, which is normally carried out over short time horizons (again, saving another 1%).

The big question is one of what is the average skill of a spread better? According to a Cass Business School report,[7] only 20% of futures traders manage to beat the market. That is a pretty low statistic and I would guess that amateur spread betters do much worse.

Tim Bennett, deputy editor of *Moneyweek*, candidly admitted in an article recently: "To be blunt, most spread betters do end up losing their money to the house."[8] Indeed, the web is full of stories of people losing large amounts on bets that go wrong – for example, see Michael Platt's story on how he lost £35,000 on a couple of bets.[9]

This area has been further clouded by the recent scandal of WorldSpreads that went bankrupt in March 2012 with the prospect of many traders losing significant amounts of money.

Given all this, spread betting does not look like a simple panacea for your missing 6% either.

KEY LEARNING POINTS:

- You cannot easily avoid stamp duty costs or the bid/offer spread, so the bulk of your efforts should go to reducing trading costs and fixed fees from your broker. Following the top 10 tips in this section will help, ie

  1. Trade online
  2. Pay no more than £10–12 per trade
  3. Beware small print costs
  4. Try to avoid ISA/SIPP charges
  5. Don't pay initial charges on funds and get a refund of any trail commission paid
  6. Don't chose funds to avoid commissions (they still exist, but are just hidden)
  7. Look at the bid/offer spread before you buy a share
  8. Trade internationally via funds if you can
  9. Trade in as large a size as you can
  10. If you do just one thing, trade less.

- Spread betting allows you to avoid a lot of the missing 6% by eliminating much of your costs and also does not normally suffer survivorship bias. However, the average skill (alpha) of a spread better is so low that it completely wipes out all these benefits (and sometimes all your capital with it).

1. Assuming you usually trade amounts of around £500.

2. But, by definition, you do not want to be frequently trading, even if the commission is lower, as you'll still pay stamp duty and suffer bid/offer spreads each time.

3. Portfolio turnover can be calculated by taking either the total amount of new shares bought over the year or those sold (whichever is less) and dividing it by the current value of your portfolio and multiplying by 100.

4. Over-trading is the term used describe a situation when someone trades too much to the detriment of their portfolio value because of increased charges.

5. Brad M. Barber and Terrance Odean, 2001, "Boys Will Be Boys: Gender, Overconfidence, and Common Stock Investment", *The Quarterly Journal of Economics*, 116(1).

6. There has recently been a book published along a similar theme: LouAnn Lofton, 2011, *Warren Buffett Invests Like a Girl: And Why You Should Too* (New York: HarperBusiness).

7.http://www.hughchristensen.co.uk/papers/Spread%20Betting%20full%20research.pdf (accessed 25/3/2012).

8. http://www.moneyweek.com/online-trading/spread-betting/three-spread-betting-myths-02816 (accessed 25/3/2012).

9. http://www.financial-spread-betting.com/strategies/lost-35000-spread-betting.html (accessed 25/3/2012).

"I've always been an unlucky investor. I chose Equitable Life to run my first-ever personal pension, and you know what happened to them. I bought tech fund star Aberdeen Technology in March 2000, one week before the dot.com crash. I bought the banks just before the credit crunch and sold them at the end of December, just before January's rebound. Every time I commit to a stock or sector, it falls 30% within a week. If I sell, it rebounds 30%, as the banks just have... I can put most of my big mistakes down to my own impatience and short-sightedness."

Harvey Jones, finance journalist[1]

12

Implications for Investors #3 – Change Your Trading Behaviour

In this chapter we look at what it is exactly that the average investors does that causes him or her to fail to beat the market, even when you ignore costs. We focus in particular on evolutionary and behavioural economics explanations for this. We propose that a pre-requisite for success is having a clear set of rules that you follow – particularly with regard to your exit strategy.

How to go green

If I asked you what would have the biggest effect on reducing your electricity costs, paying £10,000 to install a bank of solar panels on your roof or spending £200–300 switching all your light bulbs to LEDs, I suspect you'd say it's obvious – the panels of course. We are always seeing publicity about the benefits of generating your own power – and, at the old tariff rates[2] that existed in 2011, the deals were very good. We hear virtually nothing about the benefits of ripping out the spotlights that adorn virtually every modern bathroom or kitchen and replacing them, so we assume it can't be worth the effort. However, having done both in the last few months, the answer is actually to change your light bulbs.

The reason I mention this analogy is that it is just like the debate between which is more important for your investment returns: the charges or your skill? We all think instinctively that it must be your skill that is most important but, as we've seen in Chapter 9, it is in fact your charges that most affect your wealth while investing.

Back to those hot hands again

Having said that, these are averages, and unlike charges which affect different investors in almost the same way, there is massive variation in the skill level across investors which results in this slight negative skill number (see the distribution chart in Chapter 4).

There is a lot of evidence (for example, the results of those beginners competitions in Chapter 3 and Iqbal and his story) to show that, when people start investing, many lose money on their initial trades. They then either learn a better way or give up. Among those that continue, there are some that genuinely do seem to make money consistently (although never all the time, of course – think the great fund manager Antony Bolton, whose China Fund lost 38% in 2011). So what are the factors that distinguish those that make money more often and those that don't, and what can we learn from them? And what causes new investors to lose money?[3]

What they never told me

First, as I mentioned in the preface to this book, that as part of the research for it I spent quite a bit of time talking with real investors about their experiences. I tried to concentrate on people who had recently started investing. When I asked them all to reflect on their initial experiences and what problems they encountered, some common themes emerged.

Apart from understanding all the jargon and the practicalities of how you go about trading, there were five things that they didn't know which they wished they had:

1. Exactly what to buy
2. When to sell
3. To expect losses
4. The influence of the wider market sentiment
5. The need for patience

It's all in your (optimistic) genes

Before we look at these in detail, let me also share another finding from my interviews. I asked people which of a series of statements best described how they felt during their first year of investing. One word was selected by virtually everyone: optimistic.

It is interesting that optimism, or more correctly "over-optimism", is a trait shared by most investors. In fact, it is probably not just restricted to investors, but appears to be a human trait that is partly inherited through our genes. Research carried out on Swedish twins has shown that there is indeed a genetic component in our overconfidence. Indeed, David Cesarini and his colleagues estimate that up to a third of the variation in our confidence is genetically inherited.[4] So, why might there be a genetic advantage for over-optimism, as it certainly does not help share investors, as we'll see? I suspect it has something to do with enhanced self esteem (which is linked to positive mental well-being) and the fact that optimistic people are more likely to achieve something positive – as at least they try, and sometimes succeed.

But why does this inherited bias cause so much of a problem for you as an investor? It means that you will overestimate your ability to predict and control what are for the most part random events, ie, share movements. If you have success in your first few trades, you'll think you are a natural and know how to profit easily from share dealing. In fact, in all likelihood, you had in effect just tossed a coin and happened to get three heads in row. There is much more to successful trading than luckily picking some shares that happen to go up in value.

Other researchers (also using twins in Sweden) have argued that the some of the key behavioural biases which cause underperformance – eg, over-trading and loss aversion (see below) – are also genetically linked to a certain extent.[5] Again, we appear to be hard wired not to be good investors.

Bad losers

Let's look in more detail at one of the issues that cause us to lose money – that of loss aversion. In 2002, Amos Tversky and Daniel Kahneman won the Nobel Prize for Economics for showing that we hate losses twice as much as gains. Again, there is genetic hard wiring going on here. If you're a hunter–gatherer who has the option of finding some more wild grapes as a treat but potentially being mauled by a sabre-toothed tiger along the way, you're going to take the loss more seriously than the gain.

So how does loss aversion affect your share trading? It explains one of the most common investing mistakes, namely that investors tend to sell stocks that have increased in value and hold on to the ones that are going down. They fear recognising and admitting the loss to themselves and postpone the pain. Meanwhile, the loss often just gets bigger and they end up with portfolios full of losing shares.

So, where is the evidence for this? It comes from Terry Odean, who has published a number of papers on the subject.[6] In an analysis of real stock investor records in the late 1980s and early 1990s, he showed that people sell twice as many winning stocks as losing ones. Moreover, the winners they sold outperformed the losers they hung onto by 3.4% in the next year.

His studies also highlighted some other fascinating statistics. For example, on average people bought stocks that had risen 26% in the previous two years, only to find they declined by 3% over the following one. This was in contrast to the ones they sold, which showed a slight gain of 0.5% over that time. This is concrete evidence for the phenomenon seen in so many investors of buying stocks when they are too high and then selling them too low (assuming they admit their loss and sell at all, that is).

Back to monkeys again

Dr Steve Peters (a psychiatrist) reckons our problems can all be explained by being dominated by our chimp brains. In a book called the *Chimp Paradox*,[7] he translates Freud's concepts of ego, id and superego into something much more understandable: human brain, chimp brain and computer brain. He argues that our chimp brain, which controls our emotional response to problems, is significantly stronger than our rational human brain and our automated-behaviour computer brain.

In an interesting article reviewing the book, Prabhat Sakya argues this is why, when we see the prices of shares tumbling, we respond with our chimp brain.[8] It is shouting at us that the share is going to crash and to sell while we still can. This is despite our human brain arguing rationally to us that shares do go up and down and our original policy was to buy and hold.

Our chimp brain is apparently five times as strong, so it usually wins, as we've seen from Terry Odean's evidence.

Apparently, our only saviour is to exercise our chimp brain. Examples in the book include letting it sound off and getting it to discuss its actions first with our human brain (or ideally someone else) before acting.

Decisions, decisions, decisions

So, returning to the five themes from my interviews, I think this data illustrate some of the key issues. First, when new traders start, they say it is actually really difficult to know what to buy. They tend to look around for tips in newspapers, magazines and online. However, by the time these are printed and well known, the action has already taken place on the share price (as evidenced in the research on the pro's predictions for the *Wall Street Journal* we saw in Chapter 3). Moreover, they are often making decisions quite randomly and on impulse without reviewing in detail the financial state of the company or its recent share price movements.

SOME QUOTES FROM NEW INVESTORS[9]

John: WHY DID YOU CHOOSE YOUR FIRST SHARE? *"As I looked through the list in* The Times *and therefore chose alphabetically, it was probably Autonomy."*

Brian: *"The most difficult was the picking of shares. Was I going for defensives, FTSE 100, 250 or AIM? I chose a basket of shares based on my previous business knowledge. Now, over two years later, I don't own any of my original shares."*

Terry: *"I thought choosing a share to buy was going to be hard, but it was the selling at the right time that was difficult,*

> *especially a dropping price: to cash in immediately, hang on or sell some and keep some."*
>
> Carl: *"I usually just go on gut instinct. Sometimes it works, other times – yuk!!! I have really lost out by holding on too long in some cases."*
>
> Christopher: WHAT THREE THINGS DID YOU NOT KNOW WHEN YOU STARTED:
>
> *"1) At some point you will lose money.*
>
> *2) You're not as clever as you think you are.*
>
> *3) At some point you will lose money."*
>
> Carl: *"As a small shareholder, I was surprised by the volatility of the global market and how quickly it affected the value of my shares."*

Tell me a story with a happy ending

Investors, and not just new investors, are all swayed too heavily by stories. Stories are schemas that help us make sense of the world. The better the story, the more credible we think it is and the more likely we are to buy a share because of them.

As an example of how we are influenced in this way, James Montier quotes a great example of how some jurors completely abandon the evidence in favour of a good story.[10] In a murder trial experiment, jurors listen to the basic facts of a murder trial and 63% say the defendant is guilty (this is the control). If the same facts are instead presented by the prosecution using a story to re-tell events, the number saying he is guilty rises to 78%. If, on the other hand, the defence uses a story to portray its facts, only 31% say he is guilty, ie, much less than half than when the prosecution tells the story.

Some of the best examples of stories used in the investing world are for IPOs (offerings of shares in a new company). Great efforts are made by advisers to ensure the stock is taken up and the story is as watertight as possible. According to Montier, the average IPO share has underperformed the market by 21% in the three years after listing (1980–2007). We rest our case, m'lord. Therefore, ensure you focus on facts and try and ignore emotional content in stories when evaluating share purchases.

How the best of plans go wrong – especially if you have no plan!

If that is not bad enough, virtually none of the new investors I spoke with said they had any formal plan for when they were going to sell the shares. Most had vague plans of selling when they made a profit (sometimes 10%, sometimes 100%+). Others thought they would just buy and hold. Only a few operated any stop–loss procedure.

Linked to this, despite the warnings that we see everywhere that the "prices of investments may go up and down and you may lose your capital", few expected this to happen to them – over-optimism at play again. It was therefore a great surprise for many to have to deal with this problem so quickly in their investment lives.

Investing is just a game of poker

In fact, a number of the people I conversed with used gambling analogies to describe what it had been like with their initial losses. As one of them (Ann), put it to me: *"You are looking at companies and predicting that they will do well or become winners. You probably have more information than most gambling games but the end result is the same. You win or you lose."*

Only when I mentioned this to a semi-professional poker-playing friend of mine, did I fully come to appreciate how closely the two are linked. For a start, he said many of those he plays with in competitions are actually city traders. He observed that the attributes required to do both well are very similar.

In his view what makes a good poker player are two things. The first is understanding the odds and acting in a totally rational and unemotional way in the face of them. A half of pros fold after seeing their first two cards, foregoing a small loss at that point, even if they believe the odds might be only slightly against them. He contrasts this with amateurs, and beginners especially, who frequently carry on past this point, upping their stake at each round of cards, before only at the end admitting defeat with a much bigger loss.

The other distinguishing feature of a pro poker player is their ability to read *trends* (an interesting choice of words in the investing context). In the poker world, this means being able to sense when people are playing differently, and more "loosely" in particular. This might be because they've had a streak of bad luck or have got into a rage over losing a previous hand unfairly. Such trends include drinking slightly more or being more excited or nervous. All of these influence the pro player's mental model of their odds in each round and whether they decide to keep in the game or fold.

The final similarity between the two relates to our discussion on charges. When playing in a casino, it is normal for the dealer at the end of a round to collect up all the stakes, and take 5% for themselves (ie, the house) before giving the remaining 95% to the winner. The parallel and the level of the charge are spookily similar to gambling on the stock market.

M&S share price unaffected by sales of underwear

Another aspect that came as a bit of a shock for most new investors was to discover that the price of a company's share is affected not just by its profits and performance, but by overall market sentiment. Indeed, I think even old hands at trading might be surprised at how much of the variance of a share price is affected by overall market sentiment rather than fundamentals in profits. For example, I ran a simple regression analysis of Marks & Spencers' (MKS.L) six-monthly share price and its profits over the last 10 years. The correlation with the change in profit level was 0.65.[11] When I did the same correlation, ignoring any information about M&S, and correlated it with the FTSE as a whole, the correlation went up significantly to 0.85. In other words, if you knew nothing about the status of M&S at all, didn't know who they were or what it did, had never looked at its accounts or profits, you could predict with 85% certainly its share price by just knowing what the level of the FTSE was.

M&S is not an isolated example picked out to make a point. According to the CBOE measure, the overall correlation of all shares with the US S&P 500 index[12] reached over 80% in December 2011.

Zen and investing

The final thing many said they did not know when starting investing was the need for patience. Most expected their hobby to be a full-on experience requiring you to be monitoring and potentially trading all the time. Indeed, to the detriment of their portfolios, I know many of those I spoke to had portfolio turnovers of well over 200% in their first year which, as we've seen in the previous section, can seriously reduce your capital through all the charges involved. Instead, many needed to acknowledge the words of the Jesse Livermore, who wrote over 70 years ago:[13] *"After spending many years in Wall Street and after making and losing millions of dollars I want to tell you this: It never was my thinking that made the big money for me. It always was my sitting. Got that? My sitting tight!"*

The way to nirvana

So what is my take on all this and what should investors learn?

First, you need to understand your in-built behavioural biases that will cause you to do the wrong thing. In particular, work on avoiding over-optimism and dealing with loss aversion. It was shown in those studies of mutual fund investors in Chapter 4 that most investors lose money by buying and selling at the wrong times. Do not be among them.

Talking to successful investors and looking through all the research out there, it strikes me that what seems to make a good investor is someone who is methodical. You need to:

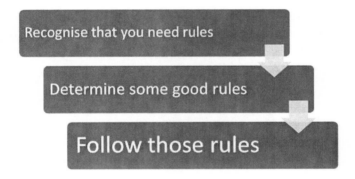

Source: monkeywithapin.com

The real life Eddie Murphy(s)

If you want evidence of the potential success of having a clear strategy, Google "Turtle Traders".[14] In 1983, when Eddie Murphy was taught and implemented a successful dealing system in the film *Trading Places*,[15] legendary commodity trader Richard Dennis copied the film and bet his colleague William Eckhardt that he could take anyone off the street and train then in two weeks to be a successful trader like him. In true Hollywood fashion, of his 14 recruits, two went on to earn over $175 million within five years.

Their secret? Religiously following a system that described when to buy and sell. It involved something called *trend following* and buying and selling on break-outs from trends. His traders completely ignored the noise coming from the media and just concentrated purely on the changes in share prices.

Risk of ruin

Another aspect of the success of the Turtle Traders is that they were taught to employ risk management techniques. He ensured they never bet more than 2% on any one trade and that every trade had a clear exit strategy (for better or worse).

This is linked to a gambling concept called the *risk of ruin*. It is the probability that you will lose sufficient capital to make it almost impossible to recoup your losses. For example, if you are dealing a large proportion of your wealth each time, it does not take make bad trades for you to reach this situation.

There is much that a private investor can learn in this area and I suggest you read more about it[17], especially if you use spread betting. Techniques you can employ include setting limits on the percentage of your wealth you are willing to gamble on a trade, working out the maximum amount you are willing to lose over a fixed period of time e.g. a day or month, etc. Note your risk is highest when you first start trading and the potential chance of risk of ruin increases the longer you trade, by definition. Remember the great Jesse Livermore lost his whole fortune a couple times during his lifetime!

Given the above, I think there is some evidence that you could learn to be one of those with "hot hands" if you are disciplined and methodical. However, note that Richard Dennis did screen his 14 recruits heavily to find those who had the most potential, so "nature" may be more important than "nurture" than it first appears in this example.

The magic bullet is...

Furthermore, I'm not advocating using the turtle trading system as any form of magic bullet. It is probably the structured principle that you need to follow. Personally, I have found it extremely useful to create a list of questions linked to your strategy and have a clear selling strategy (for both making a profit and cutting your losses). Then ensure you write down the answers to all of them before you make a purchase. Then get someone else to try and argue with you over why you should not make the purchase – ideally a woman.[16] Once you've made the purchase, frequently review this information to see if it is still valid. If the reason you bought the share is no longer true, sell.

Finally, having a clear set of rules that you follow is probably a pre-requisite for success. It will only be a success, though, if you have a good strategy in the first place. More on that in the next chapter.

KEY LEARNING POINTS:

- Most people are genetically pre-programmed with two traits that will reduce your returns: over-confidence and loss aversion.
- Over-confidence causes us pick the wrong stocks and trade too frequently.
- Loss aversion means we don't sell losers quickly enough.
- New investors often don't know five things: exactly what to buy, when to sell, to expect losses, the influence of the wider market sentiment and the need for patience.
- Successful investors: recognise that you need rules, determine some good rules and, most importantly, follow those rules.
- Creating and completing a checklist of those rules (including exit strategies) can also be beneficial.

---

1. http://www.fool.co.uk/news/investing/2012/02/07/the-link-between-luck-and-longevity.aspx (accessed 8/2/2012).

2. I'm assuming you installed them prior to March 3rd 2012 and received the higher rate tariff of 43p per unit.

3. If you want to read about this subject in more detail, I recommend you buy James Montier, 2010, *The Little Book of Behavioral Investing: How Not to Be Your Own Worst Enemy* (Hoboken, NJ: John Wiley & Sons). It is full of some fantastic examples of what investors do.

4. David Cesarini *et al*, 2009, "Heritability of Overconfidence", *Journal of the European Economic Association,* 7.2(3), pp 617–27.

5. Henrik Cronqvist and Stephan Siegel, 2011, "Genes and Investments: Why Do Individuals Exhibit Investment Biases?", Linde Institute Conference, December 6th (see http://linde.iems.caltech.edu/wp-content/uploads/2011/10/StephenSiegel.pdf, accessed 9/2/2012).

6. One of the best to read is: Terrance Odean, 1999, "Do Investors Trade Too Much?" *The American Economic Review,* 89(5), December, pp 1279–98. See also: Terrance Odean, 1993, "Are Investors Reluctant to Realize Losses?", *Journal of Finance,* 53, pp 1775–98.

7. Steve Peters, 2012, *The Chimp Paradox: The Mind Management Programme to Help You Achieve Success, Confidence and Happiness* (London: Vermilion).

8. http://www.fool.co.uk/news/investing/2012/03/07/investing-and-the-chimp-paradox.aspx (accessed 13/3/2012).

9. Interviews conducted by the author in November/December 2011.

10. James Montier, 2010, *The Little Book of Behavioral Investing: How Not to Be Your Own Worst Enemy* (Hoboken, NJ: John Wiley & Sons), citing N. Pennington and R. Hastie, 1988, "Effects of Memory Structure on Judgment", *Journal of Experimental Psychology: Learning, Memory and Cognition,* 14(3),pp 521–33.

11. A correlation defines the degree to which two or more variables are related. It varies between −1 (completely negatively correlated, ie, if one goes up, the other goes down exactly the same) to +1 (completely positively related, ie, both go up exactly the same). A correlation of 0 indicates no systematic relationship between the variables.

12. A somewhat complicated measure based on the S&P 500 index and futures contracts (see http://www.cboe.com/micro/impliedcorrelation/ accessed 9/2/2012).

13. Edwin Lefèvre, 2010, *Reminiscences of a Stock Operator* (Hoboken, NJ: Wiley Investment Classic), originally published in 1923.

14. Just Google it or read something such as:
http://www.investopedia.com/articles/trading/08/turtle-trading.asp
(accessed 9/2/2012).

15. Paramount Pictures, producer: Aaron Russo, 1983.

16. There are many reasons why I say this. For example, read: Merryn
Somerset Webb, 2007, *Love Is Not Enough: The Smart Woman's Guide to
Making (and Keeping) Money* (London: Harper Press).

17. http://seekingalpha.com/article/182985-the-importance-of-calculating-
your-risk-of-ruin (accessed 13/5/2012)

"Fashion models and financial models bear a similar relationship to the everyday world. Fashion models are idealised concepts of male and female beauty. Financial models are idealised representations of the real world.

Neither is real. Models don't quite work in the way that the real world works. There is celebrity in both worlds. In the end, there is the same inevitable disappointment."

Satyajit Das, banker and author[1]

13

Implications for Investors #4 – Review Your Strategy

In this chapter we look at what implications our findings have for investing strategies. In particular, we look at the merits of buy and hold, dividend and value investing and "technical" strategies in the current environment.

When I spoke with new investors, the one thing they all seemed to have remembered from what they learnt about investing initially was that you have to buy and hold investments for the long term. Virtually every website or financial provider drums home this message loud and clear. For example: *"Investing in stocks requires a minimum five-year time horizon…We buy stocks with the intention of holding them for the long haul"* The Motley Fool[2]

To have and to hold from this day forward…

Wikipedia defines this strategy as follows:

"Buy and hold is a long-term investment strategy based on the view that in the long-run financial markets give a good rate of return despite periods of volatility or decline. This viewpoint also holds that short-term market timing, ie, the concept that one can enter the market on the lows and sell on the highs, does not work; attempting timing gives negative results, at least for small or unsophisticated investors, so it is better for them to simply buy and hold."[3]

But let us examine the logic behind this statement in more detail. It is predicated on the assumption the market will offer a "good rate of return". As we've seen, this has not happened in the last decade. Moreover, the likes of Deutsche Bank in their 2012 report[4] are predicting real return from equities (in the US) over the next decade will be just 0.6% pa. They therefore conclude that: *"Overall, the next decade will likely be one where buy and hold will generally be a fairly poor option in developed markets. Identifying the turns in the business cycle will likely see the best chance of outperformance."*

So, let's have another story with Janet and John to illustrate the effects of what Deutsche Bank are saying.

Story #4: Janet and John take a trip to the future

It's January 1st 2012, John has read a few pages of a new book a friend is writing called *Monkey with a Pin*. Without waiting for the rest of the book to be written, he rushes off to try and ape the strategy to impress Janet. He pins up the

FT in the garage, gets his darts out and picks 20 of the FTSE shares.

He has at least read Chapter 11 as well, so he sets up as cheap an ISA as he can and sets out to buy and hold his shares for 10 years.

To work out his returns, we are going to use the model of investor returns created in Chapter 9. With it, let's assume Deutsche Bank are correct over returns being just 0.6% pa.

As ever, Janet is much more cautious and, having proved her point about her cash ISA before to John, is going to do the same again. For her, let's assume *financial repression* is again enacted by the Bank of England, and they keep base rates low for the whole of the next 10 years. I have assumed inflation at 5% pa (the other half of the repression) and a number of other things, which are summarised in the footnotes.[5]

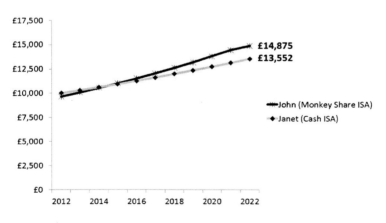

Source: monkeywithapin.com

The results are clear (or they seem to be). Despite losing some money in year 1 due to charges, John's monkey buy and hold strategy is probably going to increase his capital more than putting it in a building society over the next 10 years, assuming the current Bank of England interest rate policy holds.

He therefore and for the first time, has the last laugh. He has finally beaten Janet at investing and turned a tidy profit too – those monkeys weren't daft after all. He decides to spend some of his gains on buying Janet some new Jimmy Choo shoes as a birthday present to make up for her disappointment.

This analysis is probably fairly realistic of what people will think when they see their ISA annual portfolio statement. But, hang on, what about the effect of inflation itself? Let's also model what the purchasing power of £10,000 would have become over that period assuming the same 5% inflation.

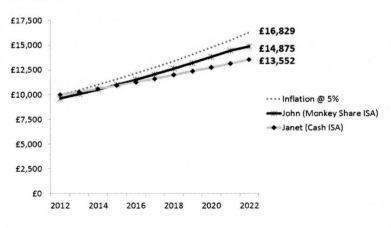

Source: monkeywithapin.com

In this light, neither strategy looks good and, whichever you follow over the next 10 years, you still end up losing purchasing power versus inflation. Note this, in my view, is a best-case scenario for buy and hold. Most investors (especially John) would not have been able to follow this through and would be likely, at one of the market gyrations where they see their portfolio halved in value, to bottle out, therefore incurring a much worse result. In addition, few in real life can resist the temptation to tinker with holdings and therefore incur further charges, again reducing yield. I doubt John would ever beat Janet in real life.

Low returns over the next decade

I know you're sitting there, thinking this can't be. However, there is an increasing body of experts in the industry now predicting low returns from shares in the near future. I'm sure you'd like to think investment returns will be greater than 0.6% over the next decade. After all, historically there have been 5%, haven't they? But remember, they were just over 1% pa[6] over the whole of the last decade and the world debt crisis has not even started to be fixed yet.

It's not just me predicting this. Let me remind you that Barclays mortgage department[7] are also assuming zero returns on stocks and shares ISAs over the next 25 years. From my calculations, I think Barclays are being a bit pessimistic – probably because I foresee greater inflation than them. However, Barclays mortgage department, Deutsche Bank and my conclusions all point in the same direction – *you will probably not make money on the stock market in the coming decade with a simple buy and hold strategy.*

Don't get me wrong, there is a lot to recommend such a strategy in the right investing environment. It would have done extremely well in the 1980s and 1990s – interestingly, this was when people most started to advocate its use. However, I suspect during that time pretty much any strategy would have worked too – even those devised by monkeys.

The "value" of "dividends"

OK, so if you don't want to follow a buy and hold strategy, what are your other alternatives? Many people talk about following dividend investing and value investing. Both of these are in fact largely sub-variants of buy and hold. In dividend investing you seek out shares that have above-average dividends. In value investing you seek out shares that you believe, according to your clever calculations, happen to be cheap at the moment. But, in both, the essence is also to keep them in your portfolio long term producing dividends and/or capital growth.

Let's look at both of these strategies briefly. Both have plenty of what psychologists call face validity, ie, they look like they ought to work. I suspect the reason in practice both largely work is because they are actually variants of buy and hold, which leverages the power of compound returns and low trading costs. However, there are some issues with both of them that makes neither a magic bullet for investors.

Where did my dividend go?

Looking at dividend investing first, the main issue is that great care needs to be taken over the selection of high dividend stocks. Dividends are a trailing measure of the company's wealth, as many dividend investors discovered in 2008. In July that year, Lloyds Banking Group (LLOY.L) was projected to have a dividend yield of 13%. They then stopped paying a dividend, and their share price plummeted. The world is full of examples of what were good dividend payers suddenly evaporating.

In his recent book, *Free Capital*, Guy Thomas reports on the investment strategy of some millionaire traders. One, a writer for the *FT* called John Lee, uses a dividend strategy called defensive value and dividends (DVD). He particularly seeks out "double seven" shares – those with a price-to-earnings ratio (P/E)[8] below seven and a dividend yield over 7%. In an article after the book was published, The Motley Fool[9] looked at what shares might fit the bill if this was to be taken literally. It included a number of companies that have since hit very bad times. For example, Thomas Cook (TGC.L), which at the time (June 2011) was trading at 128p, with a prospective P/E of 5.2 and a yield of 8.6% – ie, very much a DVD share. Subsequently, it suspended its dividend and is now trading at just 13p as I write (ie, investors would have suffered a 90% capital loss and received no dividends to boot).

I know that advocates of such an approach would argue these are extreme examples and that their screening methods would have avoided them. All I mean to point out is that dividend investing, like other strategies, is no simple guarantee of success.

Don't catch those falling knives

Value investing involves buying shares that appear to you to be underpriced. How you define underpriced is up to your own analysis, but often includes those that trade at discounts to book value or tangible book value, have high dividend yields, have low P/E multiples or have low price-to-book ratios.

Value investing done well is a good strategy – it has helped Warren Buffett's Berkshire Hathaway's returns to reach 20%+ pa. However, in practice, and for a normal investor, it is difficult to get the timing right. The bulletin boards are full of people lamenting having "caught a falling knife" that has carried on falling. Also, as we noted in the last chapter for Marks & Spencer, so much of a share price is actually determined by overall market sentiment and not by factors related to that company. This type of fundamental analysis is therefore fatally flawed in my view. That being said, the concept of buying low can be key to investment success and one we'll come back to shortly. It is just difficult to do in practice.

I just love that pattern. It's so trendy

There are many other investment strategies and too many to review in detail here. However, there are a number of which I'll group under the label *technical* strategies, as they all share a common theme of focusing on price rather than fundamentals. This includes trend (or momentum) investing, which involves buying shares that are trending higher and selling (or shorting them) when the trend switches negative. Although somewhat contrary to the efficient market hypothesis,[10] there is evidence that some shares do indeed seem to follow trend patterns on both a short-, medium- and long-term basis, at least some of the time. Certainly, on an aggregated index basis (eg, the FTSE), these patterns can be more easily seen. For example, look at the FTSE 100 since the mid 1990s:

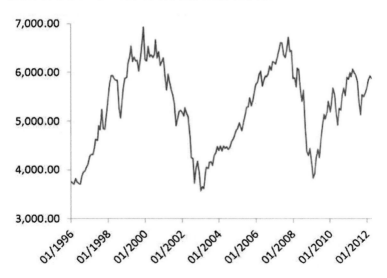

Source: monkeywithapin.com

The crosses from heaven and hell

Vince Stanzione, the self-proclaimed millionaire trader, has been saying for a number of years now that buy and hold is dead.[11] Instead, he has been known to advocate a simple system of buying shares when the index is above its 20-month (420 days) moving average and selling them when it dips below it. Others have promoted using measures such as *golden crosses* and *death crosses*, where you either initiate trades when the short-term moving average (often 50 days) crosses the longer-term one (usually 200 days) or close them/short the market on the reverse (or death) cross. There are also more sophisticated systems based on various technical analysis indicators such as the Relative Strength Index (RSI)[12] or just break-outs from chart patterns to initiate trades.[13] Still others advocate the use of patterns such Elliott Waves[14] or Fibonacci retracement levels.[15]

Like all systems, their proponents make great claims about their success. A key thing to note is that such systems can be very time-specific – ie, they are created based on analysis of back data at a specific point of time. Given this, they may not work well going forward into a different investing horizon, ie, moving from secular bull to secular bear markets. Having said that, in periods of secular bull markets (such as the 1980s and 1990s), probably almost any system would have produced positive results, even deducting 6% pa.

Now, in the current secular bear market, no system is going to work all the time (especially after trading costs). If one did, everyone would follow it and then by definition it would not beat the market. Furthermore, in real life most technical systems have limited predictive ability. Although there are many instances of them correctly predicting an event, there are also many of them failing to do so and producing false signals. As a very simple example of this, take a look at the sequence of golden and death crosses on the FTSE 100 below:

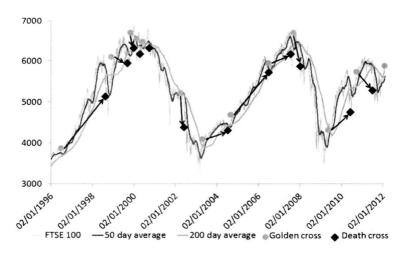

Source: monkeywithapin.com

Over the last 16 years, about a half of the golden crosses would have produced positive results and the other half false trading signals. Moreover, they become particularly unreliable at market peaks, ie, the time when arguably they would be most useful. Add to that, my analysis of trading costs (Chapter 6) suggests that this strategy will be far less effective than it appears due to constant switching in and out of stocks. Furthermore, the policy also means you are out of the market for long periods of time, and therefore miss out on dividends. Having said all that, a number of golden crosses do produce large positive returns so the net effect is probably not that different to buy and hold. Neither strategy is a simple solution to today's sideways trading environment.

Roll up, roll up – get your £500 tickets for the seminar

There are traders who claim to have made vast amounts of money using technical systems such as these (usually those keen to sell you their expensive book or get you to attend their £500 seminar). However, I suspect in reality the element they are actually teaching you is the discipline to follow a set of rules and to ensure you know how to use stop–losses. Indeed, the break-out systems are effectively ones when you gamble if the stock goes up or down. If you win, you try and make a return greater than the average loss you make on your losing gambles.

Watch those gyrations

Given the above, I have a feeling that there must be merit in trading the multi-year gyrations of indices while the market moves sideways (before its eventual next major secular bull rally). In particular, buying (and then adopting buy and hold) at a major market low when prices of all stocks are genuinely cheap is probably the only strategy that, in theory, is easy for a private investor to follow, as it keeps costs to a minimum.

Some would argue that buying at such times would be against the logic of the Efficient Market Hypothesis (EMH) discussed in Chapter 3. That states that there can be no time when stocks are cheap, as everything that is known about them is always factored into their price, ie their low price is a true reflection of their value at that point.

However you'll remember I also said there were flaws in the EMH and one of the main ones was that the market overreacts, particularly with fear. Therefore taking a contrarian view at these times, could well be successful.

So how will you know when we reach that point? Unfortunately, if there were a simple system that tells you that, we'd all be millionaires. There is none and never will be. Also, such periods are so accompanied by ones of negativity, extreme volatility and downright repulsion for shares that you have to be an extremely disciplined and far-sighted investor to take advantage of them.

Some have suggested that the best way to evaluate this point is when shares return a long-term low P/E ratio of around five. The FTSE 100 currently has a P/E of around 10. Indeed, Professor Robert Shiller of Yale Economics Department has developed an alternative method of calculating the P/E ratio that uses the 10-year average earnings based on current value (ie, inflation adjusted). The graph below shows that, in the US currently, this measure is not only above its historical average of 16 but that the market is still far away from cheap values such as five.[16]

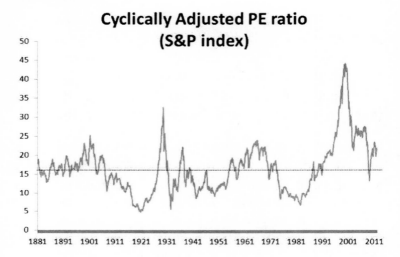

Cyclically Adjusted PE ratio (S&P index)

Based on data from: Robert Shiller, Yale University[17]

The devil's own job

If you decide to attempt to time the market bottom, you will need not only courage but luck. The last time the S&P 500 bottomed out, on March 9th 2009, it stopped at the satanic number of 666. Many traders apparently took that as an omen![18]

Or just spread your risk?

The other option that is often advocated by the industry is to never try to time the market but drip feed your investments over a period of time in a process called *pound-cost averaging*. (Ideally they just want you to set up a permanent direct debit to them, of course).

I have looked at this as a process and there does seem to be some evidence that it can reduce your risk of investing at the wrong time. Indeed part of this, as I discussed in Chapter 4, is that many people invest at market highs. Therefore if you are forced to spread your investments you largely avoid this problem.

A reader of the first edition, pointed me to a study by Bill Jones[19] which tries to quantify the effects of this approach versus lump-sum investing. It suggests it could be significant. If you spread your payments over 12 months you lose on average 2.5% vs lump-sum investing.

Therefore, I think this supports the view that you should do your best to try and time your contributions to the market at those points when you feel it is most undervalued.

Other trading systems

Finally, note that this short section cannot pretend to do justice to the vast array of trading systems being promoted to the private investor at the moment. There are many books and websites dedicated to each and there are reviews that cover them in far greater detail than I have space to do here.

KEY LEARNING POINTS:

- Buy and hold is predicated on the assumption the market will offer a good rate of return. That seems unlikely over the next decade.
- Indeed, projected returns from neither a best-case scenario buy and hold or holding cash over the next 10 years are likely to maintain purchasing power due to

inflation.

- Dividend investing and value investing are variants of buy and hold, and both have other issues.
- There are vast arrays of *technical* trading systems based solely on price analysis. None of these will work all of the time. In addition, systems are probably very time-specific, ie, they are created based on analysis of back data at a specific point of time and therefore have limited predictive power.
- The only strategy likely to be effective until the next secular bull market arrives is one of buying shares only when they are very cheap by historical standards and then holding them.
- However, defining what is cheap and having the courage to buy them then will be a challenge!
- Indeed there is some evidence that the alternative strategy of drip feeding investment money comes with a small cost penalty (vs lump-sum investing). However it can reduce your risk.

1. Excerpts from an interview by Satyajit Das by Vivek Kaul, Daily News & Analysis (DNA) (see http://www.dnaindia.com/money/interview_derivatives-business-is-full-of-beautiful-lies_1187063-2, accessed 8/3/2012).

2. http://www.fool.com/how-to-invest/thirteen-steps/step-5-avoid-the-biggest-mistake-investors-make.aspx (accessed 9/2/2012).

3. http://en.wikipedia.org/wiki/Buy_and_hold (accessed 9/2/2012).

4. http://www.fool.com/investing/general/2011/09/19/should-we-finally-bury-buy-and-hold.aspx (accessed 9/2/2012).

5. Assumptions:

i. That we use a share ISA without any set-up or management charges (not easy, but possible). I am assuming £12 commission charge on share purchases in year 1 and 0.5% stamp duty and a 0.7% bid/offer spread loss. In year 10, £12 commission to sell each share. 0.6% pa growth includes dividends.

ii. Alpha becomes zero as shares are chosen at random. However, there still needs to be a survivorship bias beta deduction of 1% pa.

iii. For the cash ISA, I have taken a typical current best rate of 3.1% and assume it will potentially be switched each year to ensure this rate is maintained. The current limit annual limit is £5,340. I have modelled in the first year paying basic rate tax on £4,660, which I assume I have put in a one-year bond with Allied Irish at 3.5% pa. It then joins the ISA funds for the rest of the term.

6. After inflation.

7. *Sunday Times*, Money section, 12.02.02, p 3.

8. The P/E ratio can be calculated by dividing the company's market capitalisation by its total annual earnings.

9. http://www.fool.co.uk/news/investing/2011/06/27/the-top-seven-7-7-shares.aspx (accessed 10/2/2012).

10. The efficient market hypothesis says that financial markets are "informationally efficient" – ie, at any given time, everyone knows everything about a company and its share price therefore reflects this. Therefore, you can't beat the market consistently over a long period of time.

11. http://420exchange.com/tags/vince-stanzione (accessed 9/2/2012).

12. For example, Frank Hassler (see http://engineering-returns.com/, accessed 13/2/2012).

13. For example, Francis Hunt (Market Sniper) (see http://themarketsniper.com/about-the-market-sniper, accessed 13/2/2012).

14. Elliott Wave theory predicts that markets follow a five-wave pattern followed by a three-wave counter-corrective pattern (see http://en.wikipedia.org/wiki/Elliott_Wave_Principle, accessed 13/2/2012).

15. Fibonacci levels are a system for determining support and resistance levels based on the idea that markets will retrace a predictable portion of a move, after which they will continue to move in the original direction. The retrace follows mathematical formulas. Key levels include: 23%, 38%, 50%, 62%, 77%, 100% (see http://en.wikipedia.org/wiki/Fibonacci_retracement, accessed 13/2/2012).

16. Note, Shiller is not without his detractors such as David Bianco, US stock strategist at Bank of America Merrill Lynch. He has created his own version of the Shiller ratio that shows it to be far less over-valued. He also feels the comparisons to the depression years are no longer valid. However, even on Bianco's measure, shares are still not cheap (see *Wall Street Journal* article: http://online.wsj.com/article/SB10001424052748704630004576248991330789506.html, accessed 13/2/2012).

17. www.econ.yale.edu/~shiller/data/ie_data.xls (accessed 23/2/2012).

18. For example, http://seekingalpha.com/article/124821-in-this-devil-of-a-market-could-666-be-the-bottom (accessed 13/2/2012).

19. http://www.efficientfrontier.com/ef/997/dca.htm (accessed 10/5/2012).

"A very low-cost index [tracker] is going to beat a majority of the amateur-managed money or professionally managed money. "[1]

Warren Buffett, business magnate and legendary investor.

14

Implications for Investors #5 – Reconsider Your Group Investment Type

In this chapter we look at the implications of our findings for the type of group investments you choose. We particularly focus on the benefits of, and issues with, holding different types of unit trust fund. We also compare the merits of unit trusts with exchange-traded funds and investment trusts. The chapter not only looks at the relative costs of these alternative group investments, but also goes into detail of how they work. Finally, we also touch on pension funds and structured products.

I'd like to start this chapter with a clear warning, to reiterate the message you read before starting this book. The information you read here summarises my deductions from the evidence in the first section and summarises the investing options as I have researched them. They are not my recommendations on how you should invest. There is no right or wrong way to invest. This information may or may not be useful to you. Only you yourself can determine what you think you should do, based on a detailed analysis of your own circumstances...

Funds – the good, the bad and the ugly

From a simple reading of the evidence presented in Chapters 7, you might be tempted to think that investing in all funds is a bad idea because of their charges. As ever, it is not that simple. To remind you, I showed that the average TER of a UK fund is 1.7%, but add to that you need to factor in the costs of portfolio turnover – ie, commissions, stamp duty, bid/offer spreads and price impact. These all probably amount to another 0.6%, making the total expenses about 2.3%. However, those are averages and it varies greatly by the fund manager and most notably also by fund type.

Luckily, Frontier Investment Management conducted a detailed study of portfolio turnover rates (and by implication costs) for different types of UK funds in 2007.[2] Their data show that emerging market funds have very high costs, mainly because the trading costs, spreads and currency costs involved in such markets are higher.

Beware funds of funds

They also suggest that fund of funds costs are also higher than many realise (average TER of 2-3%). This is the fastest-growing sector of UK funds,[3] accounting for 10% of UK funds invested in the UK. They are funds which invest in other funds and are marketed to investors as a "ready-made and broadly diversified portfolio, with one easy investment".[4] They offer simplicity for first-time investors and diversification.

So why are their charges so high? This is because you are, in effect, paying two sets of charges. The first is to your fund of fund manager to buy and sell the "best funds" for you, and then each of those funds has its own charges for buying and selling the investments within it.

Trackers are cheap and easy paths to follow

So let's look at the opposite extreme: passive index-tracking funds. The charges on these are low for a few reasons. First, the constituents of most indices don't change much, so portfolio turnover is low – typically less than 5%. That means the hidden costs outside the TER are negligible.

However, with index funds, it is also very obvious what the fund manager is charging, as people can directly compare the value of their investment at year-end with the index. Therefore, most have been forced to drop charges to a low rate on this type of fund (and, arguably too, they should require very little management to just hold all the shares in the FTSE). Given this, the average TER is around 0.6% with a number of providers recently offering them as low as 0.2%.

As an example, one of the most popular tracker funds is from Fidelity, their MoneyBuilder UK Index Tracker. It currently has around £0.85bn invested in it. It not only buys shares in the FTSE, but 25% of its assets are in futures contracts on it. It also holds some foreign shares and a tiny amount of bonds and property. It claims a portfolio turnover of just 1% (meaning dealing costs are negligible) and a TER at a mere 0.3%. Its tracking error over the last five years is –0.6%, probably because it does not buy all the FTSE constituents to keep down dealing costs – possibly a false economy given this tracking error. Having said that, remember its charges are pretty low, as are some other index fund trackers (eg, from Vanguard and HSBC).

ETFs are better, or are they?

So why do so many people[5] argue that exchange-traded funds are a better investment than funds? Let's do the comparison and see.

One of the most popular UK trackers is iShares FTSE 100 (ISF.L). Investors currently have £3.5bn invested in it. It tracks the index by buying shares in the FTSE, as opposed to using futures contracts or other "synthetic"[6] means. It charges a TER of 0.4% which appears to include almost all costs, and the gap between its performance and the FTSE over the last five years has been 0.45%. It has a bid/offer spread of just 0.03%, ie, almost nothing. However, you do need to pay trading fees on an ETF and these, as we saw in Chapter 6, can be sizable – ie, a £12.50 trade can be 2.5% of a £500 purchase.

So, on the face of it, there is actually not much difference between owning a very low-cost tracker fund like the Fidelity one and an ETF. In fact, if you are buying small amounts, the lack of trading fees with many brokers now can make a fund a better option. However, you'll find there can be other fees on these low-cost funds, so the difference in practice is not that big.

First, on a fund like the Fidelity one, you will probably get charged a small dilution levy, which is a fee charged against new people buying into a fund to cover the costs of buying extra stock for them. Second, if you use a low-cost broker like Hargreaves Lansdown, you'll also get a £24 holding fee each year for such very low-cost funds (as HL doesn't get any trail commission from the fund). This may not sound like a lot, but it is equivalent to nearly 5% a year extra cost if you have only bought £500 worth.

I have done the comparison here with a genuinely low-cost fund tracker to be as generous as possible to the fund. Unfortunately, most FTSE tracker funds are more expensive than this. For example, the Halifax UK FTSE All Share Index Tracker has a TER of 1.5%, and the Marks & Spencer Money UK 100 Companies Fund has a TER of 1.04%. Remember, therefore, if you want a fund tracker, it makes sense to get one with a low TER.

The final issue with the fund option is not knowing the price before you trade. With an ETF, the price you see is the price you pay. With a fund, you get whatever price the fund manager sets at the end of the day. Therefore, when markets are very turbulent, there could be a very wide difference between the price of your units from the point when you decide to buy/sell an index and your contract note. This could be as much as 5% or more[7] on some hectic days, ie, an amount equivalent to the total average return on that fund in a year.

Let's get physical

Before you think, "I'll buy an ETF then", don't forget they have some of their own issues. The key ETF problem can be one of risk. However, to appreciate this, you need to understand a bit more about how ETFs work. They generally fall into one of two categories: either "physical" ones or "synthetic" ones. So, what are these and what is the risk with each?

A physical ETF is one that buys shares (or a commodity or currency). Therefore, a FTSE-tracking ETF will buy shares. Some buy all the shares in it, in roughly the right proportions. However, others just replicate it by buying a proportion of the constituents. That can lead to a tracking error, but it does reduce their (and so your) costs. They seem relatively risk free you think, but not when you realise that many ETFs (and funds, as we mentioned in Chapter 7) loan out their shares to those who want to short the market.

Caught with your shorts down

For example, the iShares FTSE 250 tracker (MIDD.L) last year lent out nearly all of its shares to shorters.[8] This clearly leads to a risk for those owning the ETF. If the lenders were to become insolvent and unable to buy back the shares to return them to the ETF, it is your capital that may not be repaid in full. To help reduce this risk, lenders have to put up collateral to cover your cash according to the EU Undertakings for Collective Investment in Transferable Securities (UCITS) rules. However note that they can use pretty much any share or financial product available over the world. In addition the industry often uses this collateral for its own trading purposes in a process called *rehypothecation*[16]. Both of these add to risk. Consequently should there be a major problem in the financial markets like we had in 2008 and another bank or large institution such as Lehmans went down, it is likely that the value of any collateral would be affected. Therefore, the collateral being put up most of the time is not going to protect all your capital.

Furthermore, there is no regulatory requirement for any UK fund (ETF or mutual fund) to disclose what it has on loan and what collateral it is holding.

In contrast, the US authorities not only demand disclosure but also that ETFs hold 90% cash as collateral. The UK limit is just 20% and the UK definition of "cash" is very flexible.[9] So, you may ask, why do they do this and take this risk with your cash without you knowing?[10] They earn fees. Although some of those fees go towards keeping your TER down, up to half of the fees can be taken by the ETF company directly.

Synthetic clothes

That is one of the risk problems with a physical ETF, now what about the synthetic ones? First, let me try and explain what they are. When you pay over your cash to a synthetic ETF provider, they give it to a financial derivative provider. He then agrees to provide a return equivalent to the index for a fixed fee. He also puts up collateral to cover you in case he goes bust.

The main benefits of such ETFs are that they not only often charge lower fees but they also much more accurately track the index than physical ones. However according to a Morningstar report[17] they do so with slightly higher counterparty risks. Furthermore, the exact way in which the derivative providers do their magic, for what appears to be next to no fee, is also far from clear to the retail investor.

So how common are such synthetic ETFs? Very common; most ETFs tracking indices in emerging markets are synthetic, as are inverse or short ETFs. In particular, they are offered by European ETF providers like Lyxor (Société Générale) or Deutsche Bank. They are hardly used in the US because of regulation, and also rarely by UK providers like HSBC and Barclays iShares.

Therefore, if you want a FTSE tracker, you have a choice between a physical one that might expose you to counterparty risk from loaning out the shares or a synthetic one where the counterparty risk is the swap provider (and its trading and lending). Both have risks and it is not as simple as saying physical is better. Remember the costs tend to be slightly lower for synthetic ones and their tracking error less.

Balancing on the high wire and other safety hazards

There is another issue with ETFs that are leveraged or shorting the market (which are pretty much all synthetic ones, by the way). It is the error caused by the daily rebalancing[11] of its price. This means that if you use them for a period greater than one day, you will never receive back a return equivalent to the change in the tracked index/commodity/currency over that period. Also, I have found that this rebalancing usually seems to work against you.

Finally, one further word of warning about ETFs. Most (even HSBC & iShares ones) aren't registered in the UK. Therefore, whether they are covered by the Financial Services Compensation Scheme is debatable[12] (unlike funds, which definitely are).

Final score: a draw. Take your pick

So let me try and summarise this extremely complicated section for you in relation to FTSE trackers. If you want to trade moderately small amounts (£1000-£2,000) and you do your homework to find a low-priced fund and discount platform, it might be cheaper than an ETF because of trading costs. However more generally and especially if you're buying larger amounts or want to time the market better, an ETF may be better.

Before you buy anything though, make sure you fully understand the risk of that fund or ETF. This will probably involve you writing to the managers to clarify information from them, as data about shorting or collateral are rarely published online.

One site that tries to summarise your various FTSE tracking options is smart-beta.co.uk. However be aware it may not cover all the trackers and does not provide information on shorting/collateral.

Investment trusts – never 'eard of 'em, gov

For the vast majority of this book, I have focused on funds called unit trusts, or open-ended investment companies to give them their more technical, broader category name. This is because they are the main type of investment marketed to UK consumers.

There is another type of fund product called an *investment trust*. Briton's have £93bn invested this way. Not as much as they have in unit trusts (£570bn), but it is still an important investment vehicle you need to understand the pros and cons of.

Although they appear very similar to unit trusts – ie, they invest in similar baskets of shares and financial assets – they are different primarily because they are not open-ended, ie, they are companies holding a fixed amount of shares. The price you pay for those shares is not only determined by the underlying value of the shares it owns (called the net asset value, or NAV) but also demand for them. Indeed, for much of the time, most investment trusts trade at a discount to their NAV (sometimes substantially), but conversely they can also trade at a premium, ie, you are paying more than the total of the underlying assets.

There are some other key differences with investment trusts that should be noted. First, they can borrow money and invest it. This so-called leverage can enhance their returns when times are good but also reduce them when those bets go the wrong way. This therefore means that they tend to be more volatile than unit trusts.

Another key difference is that they don't pay commission to intermediaries, nor do they do any marketing. This is at the root of why you may not have heard much about them. Given the subject of this book, these facts make a key difference, as not only are they saving on commissions but also the firm's marketing costs.

There is also no such thing as initial charges or commissions with investment trusts. This means that the average TER of an investment trust is just 1.2%[13] versus 1.7% on unit trusts. Indeed, this average hides the fact that many trusts focusing broadly on global and UK equity can have very low TERs relative to their unit trust counterparts – the majority have TERs under 1%.[14]

However, if this is all seeming too good to be true, there is a sting in the tail. Over a half of investment trust managers charge a performance fee to their fund, sometimes up to 20% on their returns. This is excluded from the published TER. However, in practice, this missing performance fee thankfully does not normally add up to a large amount.

Be careful doing the splits
Normal investment trusts provide the ability for both capital growth and dividends. However, there is a specific

type of investment trust called *split capital* that separates these out – allowing you to concentrate on receiving either dividends or capital growth. Included in this is the infamous *zero dividend preference share*, which pays not only no dividend but no capital growth either until a set maturity date – when it pays out effectively a fixed rate of interest to the holder. I say "infamous", as such products were marketed as one of the lowest-risk investments possible, before disastrously failing to pay out *en masse* in 2001 when many investors lost a lot of money.[15]

In order to truly compare the costs of investment trusts with unit trust funds, you need to know the portfolio turnover rate. Having examined many annual reports/factsheets for investment trusts, not only is this figure rarely included, it does not appear to be consistently measured – though some who quote it do at least use the "correct" US definition. Furthermore, annual reports do not itemise their trading costs/commissions. Therefore, you are actually in an even worse state than a unit trust owner in calculating the true cost of ownership of an investment trust.

The discount price label, but with a credit card-like surcharge

Finally, unlike unit trusts, you face greater costs in acquiring them. Not only do you always pay trading fees to your broker (like ordinary shares), but you pay stamp duty of 0.5% and also suffer a bid/offer spread (though usually low). Therefore, if you are investing modest amounts (say £1,000), the total trading costs of these –

assuming you buy and sell once a year – might be 3–4% on top of the TER (and the unknown portfolio turnover rate effect).

Therefore, despite the hype about investment trusts being cheaper, they may not be for some investors. Also, the opacity of the investment trust industry makes this impossible to verify precisely.

The great British pension rip-off

You're probably wondering why personal pension funds deserve their own section? To some extent everything I have written in the preceding sections and elsewhere in this book about funds pretty much applies to personal pension funds.

However, there is one big difference: initial charges.

On virtually all personal pension funds, you still pay about a 5% charge per contribution, ie, for every £100 you put in, they only invest £95 for you. In my view, that is a charge too far and one you should seriously challenge whether you wish to pay.

You do not pay that full charge if you buy a similar unit trust fund via an online stockbroker in a SIPP. However, bear in mind that many stockbrokers charge annual fees of 0.5% pa or more to manage a SIPP, so you could find a SIPP might cost you even more than paying the initial charge of 5% over 10 years!

For more information of the pros and cons of different types of pensions, go to pensionsadvisoryservice.org.uk, and then take professional advice before you act.

Crumbling structures

A number of people wrote to me after I published the first edition of this book asking for my views on *structured products*.

These are a type of group investment which has been heavily marketed to individual investors over recent years. There are many different forms of them but most usually promise to pay out a proportion of the increase of an index (e.g. FTSE) over a period of time with some form of capital protection. However the conditions for the latter vary greatly and usually in some circumstances, you could lose some or all of your capital.

So are these worth it and do they help the private investor avoid the 6% a year that many end up missing?

On the face of it, they appear to get around most of issues. As they are essentially passive investments and the purchaser does not have much influence over what or when it is bought/sold, there will be no skill deduction. As they are index tracking, they avoid survivorship bias. Finally, most don't make any overt charges to the purchaser.

However, the biggest issues I see with them are their complexity. They are built around derivative contracts that few understand, including those selling them according to

Peter Hargreaves[18] (boss of Hargreaves Lansdown). In particular the conditions in which capital will not be repaid are often complex and probably not understood by most purchasers.

Add to that, you only get a proportion of the returns of the index. More importantly, you don't get any dividends from it (which as we saw in Chapter 2, is actually the bulk of your return). They have fixed end dates, so you can't time your exit from the market to profit most from the semi-random gyrations of the market. Finally, they are also subject to *counterparty risk*, ie if the derivative provider goes bust, you could potentially lose some or all of your capital.

Therefore in summary, although they have some benefits, I don't think these outweigh their significant disadvantages. They also fail, in my view, the *too complicated to understand* test that should be applied to all investments.

KEY LEARNING POINTS:

- The costs/charges of owning a fund vary greatly, not only between providers but particularly by sector. Some of the most expensive funds are those invested in emerging markets and the recently very popular fund of funds.
- In contrast, some (not all!) index-tracking funds can have very low TERs of around 0.3–0.4% and very few other apparent charges due to low turnover rates.
- Although exchange-traded funds (ETFs) often offer better value than funds, this may not be the case for

index trackers of the FTSE, where some low-cost funds now exist.

- In addition, if you are trading modest amounts, the lack of trading fees for tracker funds can be a significant benefit over an ETF, provided you are not trying to exactly time the market.
- Indeed, funds are covered under the UK Financial Services Compensation Scheme, while ETFs are probably not.
- There are also many potential risks in holding ETFs that may not be apparent at first sight, eg, that they often loan out their shares, resulting in counterparty risk. Many are synthetic (based on derivatives) and so also suffer such a risk.
- Investment trusts are promoted as having cheaper TERs than unit trust funds. Indeed, many have TERs less than 1%.
- However, costs to ordinary investor can be a lot higher due to trading charges, stamp duty and bid/offer spread. There are also greater risks with investment trusts due to their leverage and pricing being linked to investor demand (as opposed to their asset value).
- Pension funds charge 5% on most contributions, which may lower your return versus buying funds directly from an online broker without the charge. However, as SIPPs usually have annual fees too, the alternative could be more costly.
- Structured products avoid losing the 6% that you can suffer with many other group investments. However, investors should probably be cautious of them due to

their complexity, capital risk and lower returns (especially the lack of dividends).

1. http://www.reuters.com/article/2007/05/07/berkshire-indexfunds-idUSN0628419820070507 (accessed 13/02/2012).

2. http://www.frontierim.com/uploads/frontierinvestmentmanagement-whenisaternotater.pdf (accessed 15/2/2102).

3. http://www.investmentfunds.org.uk/assets/files/research/20110705-IMA2010-2011AMS.pdf (accessed 15/2/2012).

4. http://www.hl.co.uk/funds/multi-manager-funds (accessed 15/2/2012).

5. There are many examples (eg, http://www.marketwatch.com/story/are-etfs-better-than-mutual-funds-2011-11-30, accessed 17/2/2012).

6. A synthetic ETF is one using a financial derivative provider that agrees to provide a return equivalent to the index change for a fee. Although potentially a more accurate way to track, it comes with an associated greater counterparty risk that you will not get your capital back (see http://monevator.com/2011/05/17/how-a-synthetic-etf-works/ for a much more detailed explanation; accessed 16/2/2012).

7. In fact, there were 11 days alone between October 2008 and the next six months when the FTSE dropped by over 5% in a day. On October 10th 2008 it dropped by nearly 9% (see http://www.guardian.co.uk/business/table/2008/sep/19/ftse100.worst.days, accessed 16/2/2012).

8. http://citywire.co.uk/wealth-manager/etf-securities-lending-comes-under-scrutiny-for-collateral-risk/a546043 (accessed 15/2/2012).

9. http://www.scmprivate.com/content/file/pressreleases/press-release-scm-private-stock-lending-release-01-september-2011.pdf (accessed 16/2/2012).

10. The shorting is not mentioned on the current fund factsheet, where the fund is described as "transparent".

11. This article gives a good explanation of the problem: http://www.investopedia.com/articles/exchangetradedfunds/07/leveraged -etf.asp#axzz1mwklMhxs (accessed 20/2/2012).

12. The FSA have been asked to clarify and were unable to.

13.http://www.which.co.uk/money/savings-and-investments/guides/different-types-of-investment/what-are-investment-trusts/ (accessed 17/2/2012).

14.http://www.investorschronicle.co.uk/2011/09/15/super-cheap-investment-trusts-0Ex14HiRESvGF0hPMWJ21L/article.html (accessed 17/2/2012).

15. The author included!

16. See http://en.wikipedia.org/wiki/Hypothecation#Rehypothecation accessed 16/4/2012

17. Ben Johnson, et al, "Morningstar ETF Research: Synthetic ETFs under the Microscope", July 2011. http://news.morningstareurope.com/news/im/msuk/PDFs/Morningstar%2 0ETF%20Research%20-%20Synthetic%20ETFs%20Under%20the%20Microscope.pdf accessed 16/4/2012

18. http://www.moneymarketing.co.uk/investments/if-advisers-don%E2%80%99t-comprehend-structured-products-how-can-clients?/1029244.article (accessed 10/5/2012)

"I've been tipping [gold] for a decade. Back in the early 2000s, I did so because it looked like cheap insurance against the beginnings of a nasty credit bubble. It isn't so cheap now. But it still has insurance value. Holding gold – the world's only independent currency – gives you some protection against the incompetence and idiocy of Europe's bickering politicians. So keep it."[1]

Merryn Somerset Webb, Editor-in-Chief, *MoneyWeek* and *FT* columnist.

15

Implications for Investors #6 – Alternative Asset Types

In this chapter we look at the issues and costs of the other key asset classes apart from equities and cash, ie, bonds and commodities.

There is a lot written about asset allocation and I'm not going to repeat it all here, but merely summarise the key aspects, before reviewing the implications of costs for investing in bonds and commodities.[2]

Variety is the spice of life – or is it?

The theory behind asset allocation is that you should diversify your portfolio on the basis that the different segments may perform better or worse at different times of the business cycle. The industry normally encourages people to have the bulk of their assets in shares and there is an oft-quoted rule that you should have "100% minus your age" invested in them – ie, if you're 40, you should have 60% in shares. Furthermore, as you get older and nearer retirement, more should be in fixed-return investments like bonds (see below) and cash (see Chapter 10). The rest should be in commodities, or potentially property.

To me this is a great theory and I applaud the sentiment and logic behind it. Diversification is key. However, the problem with it in times of severe financial stress is that all asset classes become correlated. For example, in the last six months of 2011 during the fear over the euro crisis, even gold became positively correlated with shares, when historically it is negatively so. Moreover, if you know that an asset class is strongly overvalued and in bubble territory (eg, bonds), is that a good time to be holding it? Do successful hedge funds follow asset allocation rules? No, they don't normally.

I don't have all the answers for you, but I do ask that you think about these issues before religiously following the textbook theory on asset allocation. Furthermore, take professional advice to determine your optimum asset allocation for your own circumstances. This book is for informational purposes only.

007 is in debt (four letters)

As I said in the preface, I have deliberately concentrated this book on equity investment. Most people in the finance industry will tell you that bonds should also be part of any person's portfolio, as they are felt to be less risky and also historically do well when equities do poorly. So let us look at them in more detail.

First, what is a bond? It is a debt investment.

You are investing in a pooled loan to someone – a country, a company or anyone else who wants to borrow money. That bond will have an interest rate and a redemption date. They are tradable and the price you pay fluctuates dependent largely on prevailing interest rates and the likelihood of the issuer defaulting.

The key risk you take in buying bonds is that the issuer may default and either skip paying interest and/or not return your capital. They have become very topical in the news now in early 2012, because some countries are close to defaulting – such as Greece. This is a reminder to all of the risks of such investments.

The government is gilty

The main two categories of bonds used by UK private investors are UK government bonds (also called *gilts*) and corporate bonds (ie, company debt). The "Barclays Equity Gilt Study" provides us with some data on the historical returns. Over the last 112 years, while equities (including dividends) have returned 4.9%,[3] gilts have returned just 1.3% after inflation.

Equity vs Gilt Returns Over Different Time Periods (after inflation)

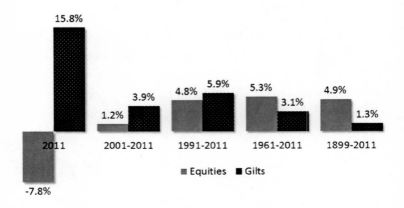

Source: "Barclays Equity Gilt Study 2012"

As per the theory on bonds versus equities, they have indeed done better over the last 10 years when shares have been struggling, with gilts delivering 3.9% pa versus 1.2% pa for equities.

The Barclays data also includes information about index-linked gilts and corporate bonds, though records do not go back very far. The performance of index linked gilts is similar to that of ordinary ones over the last 20 years.

However it suggests yields for corporate debt are lower than government debt, ie, only 1.6% pa (above inflation) over the last 10 years. This result does seem a bit paradoxical. One might have expected corporate yields to be higher, as companies are in theory riskier than countries. I suspect the comparison has probably been

212

distorted by effects of quantitative easing massively increasing gilt prices in the last couple of years. Indeed the long term (112 years) return from gilts is lower than corporate debt at just 1.3%.

When you buy bonds, you have a similar choice as with equities, of buying them directly or as part of fund, or even through an ETF. The costs/issues are similar to equity investment, ie, the charges of administering those funds or trading the investments directly mean that your actual returns will be a lot lower than the headline figures that Barclays publish. Therefore, over time, the return is likely to be negative versus inflation. However, one key thing to note is that no stamp duty is charged on bonds in the UK (government or corporate ones). In addition, charges can often also be a lower on the bond funds compared with equity ones.

Hear the bubbles popping yet?

To me the issue is not to do with costs and charges with bonds but market timing, especially for those considering investing in government bonds. Many have argued that bonds are in serious "bubble" territory. There was a very good summary of that view by Dominic Frisby in *Moneyweek* in late 2011.[4] Yields are at historically low levels, not seen since records began in 1700. The concept of *mean reversion* suggests that, over time, yields will only go in one direction from here – up. When they do, the price of the bonds will go down, ie, destroying your capital. The size of that decline could be calamitous, especially if interest rates were to rise to the levels seen in the 1970s, for example. The inflation-adjusted gilt price index lost 80% of its value over the decade of the 1970s. That's right, your capital would be worth just 20% of its value 10 years before.

Note that bubbles can carry on longer than many people think credible.[5] Therefore, it is not impossible that bonds may continue to deliver a slight positive capital appreciation in the short term if interest rates decline to almost zero. However, remember there is no historical precedent for interest rates to be lower than zero in any country in monetary history for people living in that country.[6]

Add to that, the latest Credit Suisse Global Investment report[7] shows that, in periods of inflation, bonds are the worst asset class to hold.

Therefore, think carefully before balancing your portfolio with government bonds at the moment.

On the face of it, the argument might be slightly better for currently considering investing in corporate bonds. The yield on the iShares GBP Corporate Bond ETF (SLXX.L) is currently 5.8%. That beats inflation, unlike the UK gilt rate. Furthermore, it has increased in value over 37% in the last three years. There might be some more growth possible, especially if the Bank of England continues to buy corporate debt as part of their quantitative easing programme. However, longer-term valuations like those of government bonds have to be questioned, especially if inflation increases. Also, the Barclays Equity Gilt Study show the returns from corporate bonds to have less than gilts historically.[8]

Every little helps

The only exception might be index-linked corporate bonds. A number of these issues have been made by UK companies in the last year, and they have attracted a lot of media interest.[9] The largest was by Tesco (TS1L.L) in December 2011, whose bond matures in April 2019 promising to pay not only your capital back with inflation added but 1%[10] interest along the way. Clearly, your payout will depend on what happens to inflation. In theory, if we get deflation, it could be negative. Furthermore, there is another key thing to note about all corporate bond investments: they are not covered under the Financial Services Compensation Scheme.

The Tesco bond is to help fund Tesco Bank. Indeed, some of the biggest corporate debt issuers are banks. They are a long way from having sorted out their problems, and so it must be possible that some will not continue to pay out at current rates, which will impact on both yield and valuations of bond funds like SLXX.L.

Not so Rock-solid investments

The same applies to a specific sort of traded loan made to building societies and some banks in the UK called permanent interest-bearing shares, which we mentioned earlier. The interest rates on these are very appealing – around 9% currently.[11] However, there have been a number of instances over the last few years of such building societies restructuring their loans and decreasing interest rates – eg, Bradford & Bingley and Northern Rock PIBs to name but two. If you have any interest in such shares, there are many sites out there offering advice about fixed income investments.[12] Study the risks very carefully.

Lend me 10 quid will you?

Before we finish the section on loans and debt, reference should probably be briefly made to the recent rise in peer-to-peer lending in the UK – where you can loan money directly to other individuals (eg, Zopa) or to small businesses (eg, The Funding Circle and Thincats).

Interest rates advised by these organisations for lenders vary from around 6% for Zopa to over 10% for Thincats. There are not normally lender fees, although default rates need to be factored in – currently nearly 6% for 3–4 year-old loans with Zopa, while the business loan companies don't have a long enough track record to accurately estimate them.

Again, one is reminded there is no such thing as a free lunch with debt investing.

High interest rates = high risk.

Precious commodities

Let's now look at the other key asset class of commodities. The most frequently traded ones are: energy related (eg, oil) industrial metals (eg, copper), precious metals (eg, gold), agriculture (eg, wheat) and livestock (eg, pork). For the private investor, the easiest way to invest in most of them is via a fund or an exchange-traded commodity (ETC), as many revolve around futures contracts.

The (con)tango and other ETC dances

Some of the same issues apply to ETCs in commodities as to index ETFs, ie, many are synthetic and have all those associated risks. However, there can be additional problems.

First, they are subject to a less strict regulatory environment and collateral requirements. In addition, those based on futures contracts have other potential problems. In these, your returns never seem to match up very well with what is going on with, say, the published spot price. This is because of the concepts of *contango*[13] and *backwardation*. They are both to do with the fact that the spot price of a commodity can differ, sometimes significantly, from the future price and are usually already anticipating the move you are hoping to buy into. Add to that, ETCs have to keep rolling over futures contracts and the whole thing becomes very messy, and often leads to investors losing up to 10%[14] of any gains in the base commodity.

For some commodities, like gold and silver, you can also buy physical ETCs that claim to put bars of precious metal in a vault as collateral for your investment. Clearly these have a number of advantages, as investors discovered in 2007 when AIG collapsed, nearly taking with it a number of synthetic ETCs – including commodity ones.[15]

In addition to ETCs and commodity funds, you can also invest in the companies that produce commodities. Many argue this is better as it is a more leveraged play on the rising commodity price, as it will further increase company profits. Having said that, the commodity sector of shares is full of highly speculative companies yet to produce a revenue stream. Again, do your research very carefully.

Some good bars I know

For precious metals, there is also the possibility to invest directly and buy bullion bars. A number of companies have now set up in this area to allow peer-to-peer trading of gold and silver with other investors. One of the largest in the UK is BullionVault, so let's take a look at its charges. Its trading fees start at 0.8% and decline to 0.1% dependent on how much you trade each year. In addition, there is a custody fee of 0.12% pa. Assuming you are a small investor with £1,000 and buying/selling once a year, this will add 1.7% to your costs. This is low compared with a similar transaction with a gold ETC, where dealing charges could be 2.4%[16] and typical TERs are 0.4% – ie, a total of 2.8% pa. In addition, you have the security of having potentially named bars of gold held for you in their vaults.

Trading on systems like BullionVault is not without its own issues – which are not always apparent at first. The lack of liquidity and a limited number of buyers can be an issue, and one that few are aware of. Despite them using bots that make automatic trades, there can sometimes be a disparity between prices on such systems and the spot price. This is frequently the case for silver on BullionVault, for example. Because of the lack of physical silver provided by the company, the commodity often trades at a premium to its spot value. Sometimes the gap can be as high as 5%, and it seems a greater problem when the price dips and there are potentially more buyers wanting to leverage that opportunity. Such differences can clearly impact your returns significantly.

Having said that, I have found that these exchanges have one big advantage over using ETFs. They are open 24hours a day, 365 days of the year. Some of the key price action on precious metals in the last year has happened outside London stock trading hours. If you use an ETF you can potentially miss the opportunity to buy and sell at the right time, even with limit orders.

How long can we ride on the super-cycle?

So are commodities likely to be good investments? The "story" here is that we're in a super-cycle. According to an article in *Moneyweek*,[17] there have been five major bull markets in commodities since 1792. These lasted 23 years, 21 years, 23 years, 18 years and 12 years – an average of 19.4 years. We are 10 or so years into the current bull market, so that might imply there may be more rises to come. However, others[18] have argued that the bull run in gold at least may come to a halt at some point in the mid 2010s, although possibly not until after a final bubble stage.

Another piece of evidence for "gold bugs", as supporters are called, is the 2012 Credit Suisse Global Investment report. Their analysis[19] of times of moderate inflation, ie, 3.5–18%, shows that gold is the only main asset class to perform well historically.

UPDATE (May 2012): MoneyWeek[20] is now calling the end of the commodity super-cycle, a least as far as some mining stocks are concerned (though not precious metals like gold). This is on the back of their view that China is headed for a hard landing.

KEY LEARNING POINTS:

- Despite the recent gains in government bonds/gilts, they have consistently underperformed equities over the last 112 years by a large amount, and barely delivered a return above inflation. They do particularly badly in times of inflation.
- Other forms of debt, eg, corporate debt, loans to building societies or even peer-to-peer lending, are likely to have higher yields, but have higher risk and also have other issues.
- Some believe commodities to still be in a super-cycle. ETFs are the main way private investors can invest in this asset class. In addition to the normal ETF issues, commodity ones also suffer further reductions in yield, sometimes due to being based on futures contracts.
- Those wishing to invest in precious metals can also use direct bullion exchanges. Their charges are cheaper than ETFs overall, but again can have issues.

1. *Financial Times*, November 11th 2011 (see
http://www.ft.com/cms/s/0/b323c108-0c4d-11e1-8ac6-
00144feabdc0.html, accessed 17/2/2012).

2. I have not included a section on property investment in the book. For
most private investors, they probably already have more of their wealth
tied up in bricks and mortar property than a normal asset allocation guide
might suggest. For those who don't, there are plenty of funds that
specialise in commercial and residential property, and the costs of these, by
definition, have already been discussed.

3. *Source:* "Barclays Equity Gilt Study 2012".

4. http://www.moneyweek.com/investments/bonds/government-bond-
bubble-13901 (accessed 17/2/2012).

5. http://www.fool.co.uk/news/investing/2012/02/20/beware-the-
bursting-gilt-bubble.aspx (accessed 20/2/2012).

6. In Switzerland, they were below zero briefly in the 1970s for foreign
investors to avoid over appreciation of the franc (see
http://news.bbc.co.uk/1/hi/programmes/moneybox/7809530.stm,
accessed 17/2/2012).

7. https://www.credit-suisse.com/investment_banking/doc/
cs_global_investment_returns_yearbook.pdf (accessed 17/2/2012).

8. http://www.fool.co.uk/news/investing/2012/02/13/bonds-beat-shares-
over-20-years.aspx (accessed 21/2/2012).

9. The article by The Motley Fool gives a good summary of the pros and
cons of recent ones (see
http://www.fool.co.uk/news/investing/2011/12/08/is-tescos-inflation-
linked-bond-a-buy.aspx, accessed 17/2/2012).

10. The 1% is in fact index-linked to inflation, but what they mean by that is
that if inflation goes up 5% you get 1.05%, not 5% interest!

11. http://www.thisismoney.co.uk/money/markets/article-
1583858/Permanent-bearing-shares--PIBS-rates-table.html (accessed
17/2/2012).

12. For example: http://www.fixedincomeinvestor.co.uk/x/default.html (accessed 17/2/2012).

13. http://en.wikipedia.org/wiki/Contango (accessed 17/2/2012).

14.http://www.tradingacademy.com/lessons/20110412/commodities_artic le.htm (accessed 17/2/2012).

15. http://www.moneyweek.com/investments/commodities/an-update-on-etf-securities-92624 (accessed 17/2/2012).

16. Trading commission of £12 per trade; no stamp duty; bid/offer spread is negligible on something like PHAU.L.

17. http://www.moneyweek.com/investments/commodities/money-monring-commodities-bull-market-10605 (accessed 17/2/2012).

18. http://www.marketoracle.co.uk/Article28276.html (accessed 17/2/2012).

19. Elroy Dimson, Paul Marsh and Mike Staunton, *Credit Suisse Global Investment Returns Sourcebook 2012.* Also, Elroy Dimson, Paul Marsh and Mike Staunton, 2002, *Triumph of the Optimists: 101 Years of Global Investment Returns* (Princeton, NJ: Princeton University Press).

20. http://www.moneyweek.com/investments/commodities/money-morning-mining-supercycle-is-over-21900 (accessed 10/5/2012).

IMPLICATIONS – ASSET TYPES

"The interests of Britain's millions of pension savers is not about one-year bonuses. It's about achieving security in retirement, with an investment horizon of 20, 30 or even 40 years. The real impact has been value for fund managers, value for company bosses, but no value for the real underlying shareholder – you. Collectively, the industry has failed. *It is fragmented and inefficient. It levies excessive fees. Its long-term performance is dismal. Of the 82 unit trust funds that have survived three decades, less than one-third have beaten the index."*

Guardian Money 2009[1]

16

Implications for the Finance Industry

In this chapter we examine the implications of this investigation for the finance industry. We consider what changes are likely to happen in the coming years and propose 10 ways in which the industry needs to act now as a result of them.

I swear to tell the truth, the whole truth and nothing but the truth, so where's my fee?

Writing this book has led me to the conclusion that there is much that the finance industry needs to do to live up to the basic consumer expectations of honesty and transparency. On so many occasions, systems have been allowed to develop, unhindered by regulators, which systematically allow those in the industry to profit from the ignorance of investors.[2]

I suspect it has continued for so long because the long bull run of the 1980s and 1990s, together with inflation, hid what was really going on. Only now, when shares have moved sideways for a decade, is the size of the fees relative to investor benefit becoming so apparent. Moreover, the public outrage with how the bankers have behaved since they were bailed out by UK taxpayers is only adding to the pressure for change.

Some cool surfer dudes

Some in the industry appear to appreciate the need for change. Some smaller fund groups can see there is an opportunity to surf this wave of change and actively reposition themselves to benefit from it. I'm thinking here of companies like Total Clarity Investments and SCM Private (whose slogan is "truth, honesty and integrity").

They are supported by the big US player Vanguard, which is entering the European market and also positioning its offering as "fair, transparent and exceptional value investments".

No longer feathering their own nests?

Add to that the Retail Distribution Review[3] (RDR) that promises to sweep away the covert trail commissions and make the costs of supplying financial advice more clear to the consumer.

The new employee pension scheme called NEST is also about to set a new benchmark for fees – its TER is just 0.3%, and there is an initial charge of a mere 1.8%.[4] Apart from pretty reasonable fees, there is a lot to like about NEST. Not only does it cajole people to save for their pension, it encourages them to invest in a fund related to their retirement cohort date. The decision on what to invest in is taken out of people's hands, and so they are much less likely to suffer the –2.2% losses the average fund investor loses each year purely from bad fund picking and timings.

The only sad thing about the scheme is it encourages people to put in too little. The standard annual contribution will be set at just 8% of qualifying earnings, and only up to £38,185 (ie, approximately £2,600). Furthermore, it is restricted by government statute for those who want to save more. The maximum contribution has been initially capped at £4,400 per person per year[5] (although this is now being reviewed).

To put this in perspective, consider what happens to someone when they and their employer pay in their 8% of qualifying earnings for 30 years. Assuming (optimistically) that the fund appreciates by +4% above inflation after charges, they'll still only have a pension pot of less than £150,000 in today's money value. At current annuity rates, that equates to just around £6,000 a year[6] – ie, less than a quarter of the average earnings in the UK.[7] This is just not going to be enough for most retirees, despite the employee/employer thinking they have paid in the full amount of what the government told them to.

The pinstripe revolution

My feeling is that the finance industry in the UK is on the edge of a major revolution and may well undergo a process called *disintermediation*.[8] The obvious middlemen to disappear are traditional IFAs – their main supply of income will effectively stop in December 2012 following the RDR. Few clients are going to be willing to pay fees equal to the size of their previous commissions.

I suspect the next on the list will be many fund managers themselves. As we have seen in Chapter 4, the average fund manager has an alpha of near zero, ie, brings nothing to investment choices. Along the way, however, he creates charges/fees of 2–3% pa. As awareness of this fact spreads, it will cause more and more investors to move across to simpler index-tracking funds (without such high fees).

Indeed, in a recent report by IBM,[9] it was predicted that the headcount of those responsible for selling investments will decline by 45% by 2020.

In addition, the large discount online brokers like Hargreaves Lansdown are going to have to do something about the sudden loss of the trail commission fees that will drastically affect their profits. The most obvious response (apart from charging fees on the funds themselves) will probably be to start to completely disintermediate the fund managers by setting up their own funds. Fidelity is already effectively doing this.

The final group to be disintermediated will be those involved in the pension and life fund business. For far too long they have levied excessive initial charges (as well as high annual fund fees). The advent of NEST is very shortly going to expose this in a very clear manner. At the same time, expect to see discount online brokers promote the very clear cost benefits of owning a SIPP (with them) instead of a personal pension with its initial charges.

10 ways the industry needs to change

I suspect the industry will fight these changes in every way they can. For that reason, the changes may not happen as quickly as all that. But, rest assured, they will happen. You only have to look at countless other professions to see how they are all being revolutionised and disintermediated. Think travel agents, bookshops, record shops, opticians. Even the legal profession is starting to be broken down.[10]

In the meantime, the finance industry desperately needs to put its house in order and start acting more ethically. Below, I have listed 10 ways in which I think it needs to change now.

1. *TERs.* These need to be replaced by a new measure that shows the TOTAL of ALL fees likely to be charged on funds and investments. Some have started arguing for a total cost of ownership (TCO) measure.[11] Others have suggested it be called total costs of investment (TCI).[12] It really does not matter what the industry finally decides to call it, but it does need a common word that applies to everything from an ETF to an investment trust. Most importantly, it must include absolutely all the costs a retail investor will normally pay and that could affect in any way the amount they receive when they sell. For variable costs, the latest year's audited accounts figures could be used.

2. *Portfolio turnover rate.* It is essential that this figure is known, as the private investor needs to be able to judge the true costs of ownership. It is completely unacceptable that industry self-regulators can withhold

these figures from the public. A consistent, "correct" measure should be agreed and then used by all. Moreover, its full implications (including implicit costs like market impact and spreads) need to be factored into calculations of costs of ownership.

3. *Advisor commissions.* All advisor commissions should be abolished. There may have been an argument for them when they were needed to pay salesmen traipsing the streets, but in the digital world they have become a relic of a previous era. Their existence can only bias the decisions of companies and advisers in the business to the detriment of private investors. The RDR will help remove the opacity of them for future sales, but trail commission needs to go for historic fund purchases too.

4. *Initial charges.* Although there is a good argument for a small distribution levy to ensure new purchasers' costs do not detrimentally affect existing members of a fund, this is likely to be a figure of significantly less than 0.5%. There can be no argument for charging a bid/offer spread of 5% or more on any fund now. Moreover, unless pension and life funds reform themselves, they will continue to lose business to discount online brokers and ETFs.

5. *Management fees.* There has to be some form of management fee for a fund and there will be costs associated with its administration. Currently included in the TER are also commissions, so fees will appear to decline after December 2012 when they are removed. However, even without this, many managers are still

charging too much for a performance that simply does not justify it. There needs to be a cap set on the management fee for all UK funds and the performance fees scrapped.

6. *Trading charges.* In these days of electronic trading, still charging a fixed (and relatively high) fee to buy and sell shares is an anachronism. The LSE probably charges less than 50p[13] for each trade yet the retail investor typically pays £12. There is therefore clear scope for lowering trading charges and possibly a different system based on a fixed percentage, like there is in other countries such as India. Barber and Odean report it is capped at a mere 0.14% in Taiwan.[14]

7. *Projected growth rates.* The industry must stop publishing projected growth rates of 7% pa. Although they occurred during a very abnormal period of the 1980s and 1990s, this level does not reflect current returns. In addition, all investors should be shown a projection based on the returns over the last 10 years, ie, 1.2%, as it is probably the best estimate of the next decade.

8. *Real returns (after costs).* In addition to theoretical projections for either direct share investment or for funds, another projection should always be provided based on the real returns after accounting for most likely charges – and ideally also investor alpha and survivorship bias. For a share investor, this should be based on the median share size traded by a UK private investor (probably around £1,000).

9. *Re-education of the industry.* All financial sources must be revised and include clear caveats that their projected returns are theoretical and cannot ever be achieved by an ordinary investor. These must also display results after typical charges and base their conclusions on real-life scenarios involving them. In addition, they must revise their building society comparisons to reflect accounts used by real savers.

A major mass education programme then needs to take place in the industry and be rolled out to private investors. This will probably involve re-writing almost all textbooks and online sources that talk about the benefits of investing, using more likely (and not theoretical) values.

10. *Survivorship bias.* The industry needs to be much more transparent about survivorship bias effects on decreasing returns for investors. All models that are created to proclaim the benefits of trading systems must use bias-free data. The fund industry has to stop the tricks of only opening successfully nurtured funds and also that of removing the evidence of unsuccessful ones from their databases.

KEY LEARNING POINTS:

- The finance industry has not lived up to basic consumer expectations of honesty and transparency.
- There are signs that some are starting to change, and are promoting a more transparent and ethical stance in their marketing.

- The industry is about to go through an enormous revolution and disintermediation by the discount online brokers that will see the demise of many traditional business models, from IFAs to fund managers, to pension and life firms.
- The industry needs to "put its house in order" urgently, and this chapter includes 10 detailed recommendations covering:
    1. TERs
    2. Portfolio turnover rates
    3. Commissions
    4. Initial charges
    5. Management fees
    6. Trading charges
    7. Projected growth rates
    8. Real returns (after costs)
    9. Re-education of the industry
    10. Survivorship bias

1. Guardian News & Media Ltd, 2009.

2. The True and Fair Campaign Report lists many of the recent abuses (see http://www.trueandfaircampaign.com/free-research-paper, accessed 23/3/2012).

3. http://www.fsa.gov.uk/pages/About/What/rdr/index.shtml (accessed 17/2/21012).

4.http://www.nestpensions.org.uk/schemeweb/NestWeb/includes/public/docs/low-charges-for-future-members-of-NEST,PDF.pdf (accessed 17/2/2012).

5.http://www.nestpensions.org.uk/schemeweb/NestWeb/public/NESTforE
mployers/contents/set-contributions.html (accessed 23/02/2102).

6. Assuming you retire at 65 and take a single life annuity with 3%
increases. The rate is currently about £4,000 average across males/females
(*Source:* http://www.hl.co.uk/pensions/annuities/annuity-best-buy-
rates?theSource=PPCAG&Override=1&gclid=CMG2-
86UtK4CFSMLtAodVlYERA, accessed 23/02/2012).

7.Currently £26,244 (see
http://www.guardian.co.uk/money/2011/nov/23/uk-household-earnings-
fall, accessed 23/2/2012).

8. Disintermediation is the process of cutting out the middleman (see
http://en.wikipedia.org/wiki/Disintermediation, accessed 17/2/2012).

9.http://www.ft.com/cms/s/0/3adcb3e6-5c9c-11e0-ab7c-
00144feab49a.html (accessed 28/3/2012).

10. Google Tesco's Law (see, eg, http://www.legalweek.com/legal-
week/news/2115287/leicester-firm-abs, accessed 17/2/2012).

11. Fidelity (see http://citywire.co.uk/new-model-adviser/fidelity-calls-for-
overhaul-of-fund-charges/a562275, accessed 17/2/2012).

12. True & Fair Campaign (http://www.trueandfaircampaign.com/,
accessed 17/2/2012).

13. Author calculations based on ~200 million trades a year for the LSE
(data from LSE press release showing 13.3 million trades in January 2009)
and revenue of £86.4m in the "LSE Annual Report 2011".

14. Brad M. Barber, Yi-Tsung Lee, Yu-Jane Li and Terrance Odean, 2005,
"Who Loses from Trade? Evidence from Taiwan", University of California,
Berkeley, working paper.

Paul Lewis, BBC Money Box: *"So they [TER charges] don't include everything?"*

Richard Saunders, CEO of IMA: *"Hang on, hang on, hang on. They don't include the costs of trading the underlying portfolio, and that is I think correct because the trading costs are very different in character from the costs of the fund. But…*

Paul Lewis, BBC Money Box: *"But they still come out of the investor's pocket".*

Richard Saunders, CEO of IMA: *"…but Paul, let me finish,…those trading costs are disclosed. They're in the report and accounts, which is a document I completely agree that most investors would never see. They probably don't even know it exists."*

Excerpt from BBC Money Box radio interview on February 4th 2012[1]

17

Implications for Regulators

In this chapter we examine what the implications are for regulators, and seek to understand how the state of affairs found in the finance industry could have been allowed to continue for so long.

As I was writing this book in February 2012, I just happened to turn on the radio one lunchtime and heard the conversation on the previous page with Richard Saunders, the CEO of the Investment Management Association (IMA).

Richard is not a fund manager. He is the man who oversaw the creation of the fund management industry's own self-regulatory body and lobby group that represents all fund companies. The IMA has the power to create its own industry guidelines within the constraints of EU regulation.

As an example of how this works, they issued a set of guidelines called the "Statement of Recommended Practice (SORP)",[2] which controls how the fund industry reports to investors. In their latest revision, issued in October 2010, they changed a few things and in particular removed the need for any fund company to disclose their portfolio turnover rate (as you'll remember from Chapter 7, a figure that tells you how much a fund really costs you as an investor).

When is a consultation, not a consultation? When it is an inside job

How did they go about removing it? They ran a consultation. Who did they ask? Well, 11 people within the fund industry and accounting profession. Did they consult any private investors who might be affected? No.

In their consultation review document,[3] they justify removing PTR on the grounds that it is such a crude measure.[4] This is true, but who endorsed that bizarre definition a few years earlier? They also say that "users of financial statements are more interested in the timing of transactions and the associated costs than the volume as a measure of the fund managers' skill." So how exactly did they arrive at such a conclusion without consulting a private investor?

Who is looking after the sheep?

I raise this as an example to illustrate the old adage of putting a wolf in charge of herding the sheep. Where such substantial amounts of money are involved (approximately

£10,000,000,000 per year in disclosed TER fees alone in the UK), there has got to be some form of independent regulation, or at least extremely tight overseeing to prevent abuse.

Theoretically, we have the FSA regulating the finance industry. I say "theoretically", as it could be argued that they are not looking after the private investor in relation to the fund industry either. In 2000, they commissioned and published their own internal report into fund charges, which highlighted the problems of the PTR and the fact it meant that expenses were being radically underestimated by the fund industry. To reiterate the quote[5] from it used in Chapter 6, *"Retail investors cannot easily measure the price of investing through the investment funds, in part because a significant element of this price is mostly not disclosed at all."*

So what action has the FSA taken since 2000 in relation to informing private investors of these hidden costs?

Given that the FSA knew about these hidden charges, what impact did they have over the IMA's and the EU's decisions (see below) to prevent investors from being able to estimate these charges?

Was there any governmental oversight of what the FSA was doing in this respect?

Indeed, if you look closely at the regulatory documents provided by the FSA[6] and the IMA SORP, you'll find that their wording is remarkably circular on reporting requirements. One says it is doing what the other asks, and *vice versa*. But who is making the decision and in whose best interest?

A good example of these decisions is the fact that the ISA rules were set up so that they were biased towards contributions into stock ISAs, where the industry made more money. Not only can you still put twice as much into a stock ISA as a cash ISA, but you are only allowed to transfer one way from a cash to an equity one. Why is this? It is not a system that a private investor would have wanted or created. It only benefits the industry (who probably lobbied heavily for it).

Who is Europe KIIDing?

The regulatory environment is arguably now even more complicated following the creation of the European Securities and Markets Authority (ESMA), which was hastily created in the wake of the 2008 financial crisis. This now issues directives to member states. Indeed, it could be argued that it was their removal of the PTR from the Key Investor Information Document (KIID) guidelines that sealed the fate of disclosure of this measure in the UK. The previous EU guidelines created in 2004 were very clear that PTR must be included in the Simplified Prospectus for investors[7] so they could use it to gauge costs.

So who runs this ESMA? It is an independent body of financial experts to the EU. A key element is a stakeholder group. According to the ESMA website, it "is made up of 30 stakeholders from various areas, representatives of different industry sectors, academics and retail investors".

So how many of the hand-chosen members of the 30 strong group listed opposite this statement on their website are just individual retail investors? The answer is zero (see the list at http://www.esma.europa.eu/SMSG).

To quote my local ch_ch: Who is missing? UR

To me, this is the crux of this whole problem of self-regulation in the finance industry. The key stakeholder (ie, you, the person with the money to invest) is missing from it. I am a mere individual investor with no financial knowledge, no economics degree and no experience of the industry. However, what I, and other investors like me, could easily do is ask some very simple questions from our perspective (like what is this fund costing me exactly please?) and seek out some simple and truthful answers.

Moreover, the consumer is also missing from the regulatory environment too. ESMA recognised the need to include them as a stakeholder and then didn't. I suspect the new Financial Conduct Authority (FCA), due to replace the FSA in 2013, will do the same. This is despite the government's remit to them to "be more outward-looking and engaged with consumers than the FSA has been".[8]

Getting rid of the EU's smoke and mirrors

For example, the first thing we (the investors) would do is to revisit the 2001 EU UCITS directive. It stated the need to clearly and simply disclose all charges for customers. Let's rip up the EU's smoke and mirrors with TER and PTR.

Also rip up the KIID, son of the Simplified Prospectus, and let's start again with a blank sheet of paper.

On that paper we need to write down (and itemise) *all the actual costs*, including trading commissions, stamp duty, etc, from the last year's accounts. There may need to be deduction for the distribution levies paid against them to correctly reflect inflows. Clearly, it will not include the effects of price impact and bid/offer spread. However, they could be easily estimated from a standard formula.

We'd then have, for the first time, a genuine summary of the real visible costs of running a fund. Moreover, the consumer would expect to see this total charge number go down as the fund total value goes up (not the opposite, as we saw in Chapter 7).

My views are also those of most investors. In a survey of 2,029 UK adults conducted in December 2011,[9] 89% agreed that fund managers should be required to make a full disclosure of ALL fees.

Follow the Zeitgeist[10]

I'm pleased to see that in the last few weeks I don't appear to be the only one seeking change. On February 1st 2012, trueandfaircampaign.com was launched.[11] The campaign's manifesto demands that the UK government force fund providers to be 100% transparent and publish all their fees in an understandable format.

They are proposing a simple form (see below) and encouraging all private investors to print it out and ask their fund company to complete it for them.

This concept should be taken wider than just the fund industry, with the same form being used for all investments – be they ETFs, pensions or investment bonds. I also think that it probably needs to be simplified for the general public. Most people don't care too much where the fees are going, they just want to know what will be the bottom-line effect of all of them on their investment returns.

The US regulator (FINRA) has created a website that tries to do this.[12] You select your fund, tell it how much you are going to invest and over how long, and you can immediately see the impact of costs on your returns.

	% pa	Notes (All calculations based on minimum required investment or actual size of investment where known)
% Annual Management Charge (AMC)		This should include VAT where payable by most investors.
% Custody & admin costs etc		
% Performance fee		Based on latest 12 months disclosed performance fee or average of up to three years if data available.
% Dealing costs		Based on latest 12 months or average of up to three years if data available. Dealing costs = Portfolio Turnover Rate X estimated full cost buying/selling underlying assets. Most funds will simply use a common agreed schedule of costs (see notes).
% Any other costs not included above		E.g. extra costs of underlying funds when investing in a "fund of fund" structure if not already included above.
Less any other recurring revenues		E.g. net securities lending revenues or other recurring income received based on last 12 months or average of up to last three years if data available. For example if investing in a Company pension fund, the net annual contribution to the fund being made by the employer should be incorporated. Similarly, if tax costs/benefits for the particular investor are to be included they should be added here.
Total Provider Cost (TPC)		
Platform fees via Sales Channel A		Where not already included in above figures.
Entry / Exit costs via Sales Channel A		Any charges (where one off) should be amortised over five years as the assumed length of investment unless stated otherwise. Any costs associated with a particular wrapper e.g. the initial set up costs of a fund, portfolio, SIPP etc. should be included.
Advisor fees/rebates or any other costs/recurring revenues not included above		Any charges (where one off) should be amortised as per above. Similarly, if tax costs/benefits for the particular investor are to be included they should be added here if not already included above.
Total Cost of Investment (TCI) via Sales Channel A		

Source: trueandfaircampaign.com

I sincerely hope that someone reading this has the power to say to the finance industry and their supposed regulators: "enough is enough". From now on, some honesty and respect for your end-client is required.

Moreover, someone independent of the finance industry has to be involved in its regulation.

KEY LEARNING POINTS:

- The finance industry is largely self-regulated, despite the enormous sums of money involved and concomitant risks of abuse.
- The theoretical overseers in the UK, in the form of the FSA, do not always appear to be regulating the industry in the best interests of the investor.
- Even the European regulatory body (ESMA) has no representation from individual investors, despite it being specifically in their mandate.
- There needs to be a complete rethink on charges to ensure the consumer receives one simple measure that includes ALL costs actually incurred by financial offerings such as funds.

1.http://news.bbc.co.uk/1/shared/spl/hi/programmes/money_box/transcripts/money_box_04_feb_2012.pdf (accessed 18/2/2012).

2. http://www.investmentuk.org/policy-and-publications/industry-guidance (accessed 17/2/2012).

3. http://www.investmentfunds.org.uk/assets/files/press/2010/SORP2010-invitationtocomment.pdf (accessed 17/2/2012).

4. There has indeed been some agreement in the press that the definition they have been using for PTR was maybe not ideal. However, why did they not just change it to one like that used in the US that was better? (see http://www.morningstar.co.uk/uk/news/articles/100747/We-Will-Miss-Portfolio-Turnover-Rates.aspx for a more detailed discussion of this, accessed 17/2/2012).

5. FSA, "The Price of Retail Investing in the UK" (http://www.fsa.gov.uk/pubs/occpapers/op06.pdf, accessed 1/2/2012).

6. http://fsahandbook.info/FSA/html/handbook/COLL/4/5#D435 (accessed 15/2/2012).

7.http://www.fsa.gov.uk/library/communication/pr/2004/101.shtml (accessed 23/02/2012).

8. http://www.fsa.gov.uk/static/pubs/events/fca_approach.pdf.

9. ICM Research Omnibus conducted for SCM Private (see http://www.trueandfaircampaign.com/wp-content/uploads/2012/02/True_and_Fair_Campaign_Research_Report_February_2012.pdf, accessed 28/3/2012).

10. Zeitgeist is "the spirit of the times", a phrase often used to describe the phenomenon of many people in different places all thinking the same way in the same era.

11. Download their full report here: http://www.trueandfaircampaign.com/free-research-paper/ (accessed 24/2/2012).

12. http://apps.finra.org/fundanalyzer/1/fa.aspx.

IMPLICATIONS FOR REGULATORS

"If it's interesting, it's wrong."

Pete Comley, market researcher, 1981

18

Concluding Thoughts

In this last chapter, I'll attempt to bring the whole book together. I'll give you my take on it all, what I've learnt and how it is probably going to change the way I personally invest in the future.

My first week at work

One of the first things I learnt when starting my professional career as a data analyst in market research was the maxim on the previous page. I can't remember what project I was working on,[1] but as a new trainee I excitedly went into my boss's office one afternoon telling him about this amazing finding. As I was trying to persuade him to major the whole presentation on it, he got out the raw data tables and checked my figures. I had erroneously copied 17% as 71%.

As I walked back to my desk in shame and embarrassment, I vowed to learn from this and created the above maxim. It has held me in good stead throughout the years and I've lost count of the number of times I've applied it in my both my professional and private life.

Why interesting stuff can be wrong

At its core, the quote is a belief that one should question any data. If it seems too good to be true, or against what you would expect it to be, it could be incorrect in some way. I found that sometimes the difference can be due to an error – a good example from this book is the way the industry has defined portfolio turnover rate, which seems just wrong to the average investor.

At other times, I have found it is because people have not interpreted statistics correctly, either through their lack of understanding of basic statistical concepts (eg, survivorship bias) or their inability to show the correct bigger picture (eg, the industry figures not being flagged as theoretical and are impossible for an investor to achieve).[2]

Sometimes these errors occur genuinely by accident or ignorance. Sometimes they are deliberate and put out there as part of a spin to make a point by someone wanting to sell you something, influence your thinking or get you do something. It is possible that the industry's concentration on theoretical returns falls into this category.

Dum de dum dumb?

News broadcasters these days seem to just read the lobby group press releases without seriously thinking about what has been written and whether it really can be true. Is it surprising that ordinary people (ie, us investors) don't challenge things either? We all live such complicated lives that there just isn't the time to question everything told to us. Has the media been so dumbed down that they don't feel the audience is up to appreciating a certain level of critical analysis and debate?

I was therefore not surprised, but nevertheless slightly depressed, to see how little the UK public is currently aware or concerned about the effects of charges on their investments. According to a report published by the FSA, less than a quarter of consumers buying funds even consider charges at all.[3] This issue has to be moved up their agenda somehow.

But not all interesting stuff is wrong

Don't get me wrong regarding my cynicism over data. Some startling facts are true – not least those revealed by David Kuo in the podcast that caused me to write this book. 85% of professional fund managers don't beat the market.

I've learnt a lot

Indeed, I've learnt many other surprising facts about investing while writing this book. I hope they will make me a better investor and sincerely hope that they do the same for you, and that you feel the last few hours reading have been useful. So, what are the key things that have most stood out for me?

- I genuinely did not expect to find *the odds being so heavily stacked against me* making any money in the current investing climate. In that context, I actually feel my meagre profits recently have actually been pretty good.

- I have learnt the importance of *challenging my own biases* and schema of the finance world. For example, I've tended to use ETFs and often shunned funds, but not any more. There is a place for both in my portfolio now.

- Understanding all about cognitive biases and why we seem to be *hard-wired the wrong way* as investors will help. In particular, I have vowed to create a clear trading system, write it down and follow it.

- I'll not be so prone to think that *cash in the bank is a waste*. The grass is not any greener of the other side of the investing fence on average – at least at the moment.

- I was fascinated to find out that the financial world seems to revolve around *very long cycles of about 32 years* – approximately 16 years of boom times for investments followed by a similar period of consolidation. (Though why these are called "secular" bull and "secular" bear markets still eludes me.)

- I did not realise how much investing was like playing *poker*, even down to the amount the house takes from your winnings. (Looks like I might be taking up a new hobby?)

- I'll always be indebted to *Terry Odean and Brad Barber* for doing some fantastic analysis of real investors' trading behaviour. Their painstaking analysis of billions of transactions has taught the world so much (or it should have done; they've just not been listened to yet).

- The *complexity (and size) of the charges*, commissions and fees the industry astounded me. You don't want to know how many times I've had to rewrite that section, as I discovered more and more.
- I was initially appalled when I first found *the story of the guy who'd made no money* on his pension after 15 years. I just wonder how many more people like him there are out there? Worse still, many probably don't know or realise how poorly their investments have performed. Perhaps it is lucky few are able to work out what their inflation-adjusted returns have been.
- Even now, I cannot believe why no-one has previously challenged the industry over *publishing theoretical returns that can never be achieved by real investors*. It is going to take a lot of re-education to undo those errors, as the false conclusions based on them pervade the whole industry.
- I might be wrong with my analysis of the future for the industry, but if I'm not, it is going to be bleak time for many as they gradually get *revolutionised and disintermediated.*
- The lack of independent oversight of an industry profiting so mercilessly on less knowledgeable investors surprised me. Given the stakes and staggering amounts of money involved, *self-regulation is surely not an acceptable model?*
- And, finally, how those *monkeys with pins* (or the dart throwers on the *Wall Street Journal*) manage to beat the average investor (and pros) will never leave me. Indeed, the next time the market takes a serious plunge and I buy shares again, I am going to get my

darts out and follow it. I'll let you know how the monkey portfolio does.

I'm going to finish with a staggering statistic. The total cost to UK savers of this missing 6% is about £170bn[4] a year. That is more than the UK budget for the health service and education put together. It's also nearly £3,000 a year for every man, woman and child in the UK. That's a lot of money the finance industry makes from us.

You can follow me on Twitter @petecomley or leave your comments and observations on this book at monkeywithapin.com. Also, please tell your friends they are welcome to download it for free from there.

Pete

1. I have a feeling the project was for Atlantic Container Lines – all about international shipping.

2. Given that I'm not involved in the finance industry myself, I may well have fallen foul of this somewhere in the book, so please tell me if I have.

3. http://www.fsa.gov.uk/pubs/other/cra_report_benefits.pdf accessed 20/2/2012. Note the survey in this report found 28%, but respondents were warned in advance the whole project was about charges and so this will have exaggerated the number substantially. Indeed, a previous survey in the *Sandler Review* found just 14% looked at charges.

4. The total value of UK financial assets are £4.3tr, according to ONS (see http://timetric.com/index/hMIQKlZfSZ2I1vr4MTvixg/). Of these, according to a recent survey by Lloyds Banking Group (http://www.lloydsbankinggroup.com/media/pdfs/halifax/2010/50Yearso fSavingsReportFINAL.pdf), 13% are held in shares and 54% in the form of pensions and life insurance. That makes £2.9tr, of which 6% per year are missing, ie, £174bn. If you think this figure is far-fetched, it is lower than

estimated by IBM (see http://www.ft.com/cms/s/0/3adcb3e6-5c9c-11e0-ab7c-00144feab49a.html#axzz1fZKXOXSN).